AllanBakes
REALLY GOOD CAKES

AllanBakes
REALLY GOOD CAKES

WITH TIPS AND TRICKS FOR SUCCESSFUL BAKING

Allan Albert Teoh

DEDICATION

This book is dedicated to the memory of my late mother, Mdm Ong Su Wha, my family members, especially GB and Chia, Raj and family, my local and overseas friends and last but not least, my customers, near and far. Without you, AllanBakes would not have flourished and this book would not be possible.

Compiling this book has been an arduous affair but it has also been a rewarding process. I sincerely hope that you will enjoy the recipes in the pages that follow.

CONTENTS

Acknowledgements 8

Introduction 11

Equipment 13

Ingredients 17

Light and Spongy
Sponge Cakes 22
Chiffon Cakes 38

Sitting Pretty
Cupcakes 52
Muffins 68

Old Fashion-No Nonsense
Loaf Cakes 84
Chocolate Cakes 98
Fruit Cakes 110

Super Scrumptious
Brownies 124
Cheesecakes 136

Weights and Measures 143

ACKNOWLEDGEMENTS

I would like to thank Marshall Cavendish International (Asia) for making this book possible. Thank you, Lydia, for finding and believing in me.

I would also like to thank the many others who helped, supported and encouraged me to bring this book to completion.

First and foremost, I thank my family members especially my eldest sister, Lay Choo, for teaching me to use the finest ingredients that I can find to bake better products; YC for his support and advice; GB for her constant understanding and unconditional love.

My sincere gratitude also goes to those who are always there whenever I need help, especially Ben, Beng Kiat, Harbans, Helen, Jacqueline and Susan.

Heartfelt thanks also to Kirby Kwek, owner of Stew-arts for allowing me to use his studio without hesitation when he was approached.

I am also grateful to my nieces and nephews, friends, customers and neighbours who happily lend themselves to test all my recipes.

Special thanks also to Raj and his family for being there when I needed feedback and frank opinions, friends from England for their constant encouragement as well as friends from USA who share my vision.

Last but not least, I want to acknowledge and thank those whose names I did not mention here—you know who you are. Thank you for helping me in your own little ways and for showing me how to have a balanced lifestyle.

Allan Albert Teoh

If you are an aspiring baker like I was, let your little successes spur you on and never let failed attempts bring you down.

INTRODUCTION

For me, baking has always been a relaxing and therapeutic affair, and whenever I am complimented on a batch of cookies or a cake that I have just baked, the joy and satisfaction that I feel is simply indescribable. This was one of the factors that spurred me on to start AllanBakes, my café-cum-cake shop.

If you are an aspiring baker like I was, let your little successes spur you on and never let failed attempts bring you down. Use the recipes in this book to help you build up your own baking repertoire. Some of these recipes may look lengthy and complicated, but they are not. I have carefully worded every recipe to make it easy to follow and understand. Baking a good cake is not about finding the right recipe or having the right skills. It requires patience, constant practise, a good dose of passion and of course, quality ingredients. Once you have all this in place, you will be rewarded for the many hours spent in the kitchen.

I will always treasure what my late mother once told me some 30 years ago now. She said, "No cake bought can be compared to the one you bake for me, whether it is a success or failure on your part." It is with her encouragement and belief in me that I am able to continue to meet the demands of my customers through baking.

As with any project, it is important to get your foundation right before starting, so read through the next few pages on Equipment and Ingredients before you begin. And remember to read and understand the recipe and do the necessary preparations before you embark on your baking journey.

Happy Baking!

EQUIPMENT

Baking Pans

Invest in good quality baking pans as this will ensure more even baking to help you achieve the best results. Choose light coloured pans over dark coloured pans as darker colours tend to conduct more heat, causing the base of your product to brown more quickly. A good range of pans to have on hand are: loaf pans, pie/tart pans, cake pans in various shapes (round, square, rectangle), springform pans (used for cheesecakes), tube pans (used for chiffons) and baking sheets (used for cookies or Swiss rolls).

Cake Tester

A cake tester is a thin metal skewer used for testing if baked goods are done. It is inserted into the middle of a cake, then withdrawn. If the tester comes out clean, the cake is done. However, some cakes like fruitcakes and brownies will still be a little sticky in the middle even though they are done.

Cutters

These come in all shapes and sizes and are useful for cutting cookie doughs or scones. Cutters should have a sharp edge so that they can cut through the dough easily. My personal preference is for metal cutters.

Double Boiler

Double boilers are made up of two pots, one fitted into the other. The smaller pot holds the ingredients while the other pot holds water for simmering over the stove to melt ingredients gently, such as chocolate and butter.

Food Processor

A food processor usually has different blades and attachments that enable the machine to perform the different functions of puréeing, grating and chopping. This is a useful gadget for baking. Choose one with a powerful motor that will enable you to work with even the hardest of nuts.

Grater

This handheld kitchen utensil allows you to grate or shred food into fine pieces. There is also a fine grater that allows you to grate zest from citrus fruit.

Kitchen Scale

If possible, get a digital kitchen scale as it would offer more precise measurements. Always set the empty container on the scale, then set scale to zero before placing the ingredients in to be weighed.

Measuring Cups

Liquid measuring cups allow you to measure liquids. Place the measuring cup on a flat surface and pour in the liquid until it reaches the desired mark/level. It is important that you take the reading at eye level to ensure accuracy.

Dry measuring cups usually come in a set of four: $1/4$ cup (60 ml / 2 fl oz), $1/3$ cup (85 ml / $2^1/_2$ fl oz), $1/2$ cup (125 ml / 4 fl oz) and 1 cup (250 ml / 8 fl oz). They are used for measuring dry ingredients such as sugar and flour. Fill the dry measuring cup right up to the top, then level it off across the top with a knife. Do not compact the ingredient into the cup.

Measuring Spoons

Like dry measuring cups, these come in a set consisting of: $1/8$ tsp, $1/4$ tsp, $1/2$ tsp, 1 tsp, $1/2$ Tbsp, 1 Tbsp. Measuring spoons can be used to measure both dry and wet ingredients.

Mixer (Handheld or Stand Mixer)

Mixers make baking tasks like creamy and whipping easier, but there are many different brands of mixers available and different brands means different speeds, so get to know your own mixer. Stand mixers are heavy-duty machines and they usually come with a paddle, whisk or dough hook. Handheld mixers are not as sturdy as stand mixers but they are great for small jobs like mixing and whipping ingredients that require being heated on a stove.

Mixing Bowls

It is useful to have different sizes of mixing bowls on hand. Having the right size of bowl for a particular recipe is important as it will help reduce the time needed to mix, beat or whisk the mixture. Mixing bowls can be made of plastic, glass or stainless steel. Of these three types, stainless steel is the easiest to wash and is most suitable when whipping egg whites.

Rolling Pin

Rolling pins come with or without handles and can be made of wood or metal. Rolling pins are useful for rolling out doughs as well as for crushing biscuits.

Sieve/Sifter

These are used for aerating and combining dry ingredients. Sieves can be made of plastic or metal and can come with or without handles. Dry ingredients are pushed through the thin nylon or wire mesh to aerate the ingredients and remove any lumps.

Spatula

Spatulas are made of metal or plastic. They enable you to scrape batter down the sides of mixing bowls to ensure even mixing, and fold flours or meringues into beaten batters lightly and evenly.

Wire Cooling Rack

Cooling racks come in different sizes and shapes. It is good to have a few large rectangular ones that can accommodate a few batches of baked products. Wire racks aid cooling by allowing air to circulate on all sides of the baked goods.

INGREDIENTS

Baking Powder

This is a chemical leavening agent that is used to add volume and texture to baked goods. Baking powder is usually made up of bicarbonate of soda, cream of tartar and corn flour. The corn flour helps to absorb any moisture and prevents any leavening action from taking place until a liquid is added to the mixture. The chemical reaction continues when the batter is heated in the oven.

Bicarbonate of Soda

Also known as baking soda, bicarbonate of soda is a chemical leavening agent used to help baked goods rise with the release of carbon dioxide. Unlike baking powder which is mixed with other salts such as cream of tartar and sodium aluminium sulfate, bicarbonate of soda is pure sodium bicarbonate. It starts to react and release carbon dioxide as soon as it comes into contact with moisture. Batters using bicarbonate of soda must be baked almost immediately.

Butter/Oil

I prefer to use unsalted butter when baking as it gives me better control over the amount of salt added to the baked product. Unsalted butter also tends to have a longer shelf-life. I do not use margarine in my baking as butter imparts a much better flavour to baked goods. In those recipes where cooking oil is used, choose an oil with a mild flavour such as corn or canola oil.

Buttermilk

Buttermilk is creamy and rich and it lends a unique flavour to baked products especially cakes and cookies. Natural buttermilk is the liquid that is left over after churning butter, but today, cultured buttermilk is also available. To make your own buttermilk, place a tablespoonful of freshly squeezed lemon juice in a bowl. Add 250 ml (8 fl oz / 1 cup) fresh whole milk and let it stand for about 10 minutes for the milk to curdle. Your home-made buttermilk is now ready for use as required in the recipe.

Cream Cheese

Cream cheese is a soft cheese made from cow's milk and contains at least 33% milk fat. When making cheesecakes, choose regular cream cheese for the best result as low-fat cream cheese does not hold up well when thawed. To store cream cheese after opening, use a resealable plastic bag and squeeze out as much of the air as possible before freezing it. Frozen cream cheese will keep for up to 3 weeks. Note however that the taste and texture of cream cheese may change slightly with freezing.

Cream of Tartar

Cream of tartar is an acidic salt typically used in baking to stabilise and give more volume to beaten egg whites. It is one of the components of baking powder.

Eggs

Eggs act as a binding and leavening agent in baked goods while providing colour, texture and flavour at the same time. Always use good quality fresh eggs and bring them to room temperature before using in a batter. Cold eggs will cause the batter to curdle, resulting in a baked product that may be grainy or flat. In these recipes, large eggs weigh approximately 68 g and medium eggs weigh approximately 58 g.

Flour

Flour gives structure to most baked goods. Commonly used flours are plain flour (all-purpose flour), self-raising flour and cake flour. All of these flours are readily available in local supermarkets. The different types of flour vary in their protein content and this affects the outcome of the final baked product, so as much as possible, use the type of flour recommended in the recipe.

Gelatine

Gelatine used for cooking comes in the form of sheets or powder. This colourless thickening agent forms a jelly-like substance when mixed with water and then cooled. Although gelatine is derived from boiling the bones, tissue and organs of animals, vegetarian gelatine is now also available, made from agar-agar, arrowroot or kudzu. I prefer using gelatine in powder form as it is more easily measured. Read the label when purchasing gelatine as the strength may vary from manufacturer to manufacturer.

Milk

Milk adds flavour and moisture to baked goods. My preference is to use fresh whole milk when baking as it produces the best flavour and texture, but reduced fat milk can also be used without affecting the taste and texture too much.

Nuts

Nuts add taste and character to baked goods. Use raw unsalted nuts, then shell if necessary and roast to enhance their colour and flavour before using. Nuts have a high fat content and tend to turn rancid easily. To keep them from turning rancid, store nuts in airtight containers in a cool, dry place. Freezing nuts will help lengthen their shelf-life.

Sour Cream

Sour cream is a smooth and thick cream that adds richness and a tangy flavour to baked products. If sour cream is not available, a good substitute is whole milk yoghurt. Alternatively, add 3 Tbsp butter to 200 ml buttermilk and use in place of sour cream. Note that such substitutions will result in flavour variations but it is always good to experiment and see what you can come up with!

Sugar

The role of sugar in baking is not just to add sweetness, but also tenderness and moisture to baked goods. White granulated sugar is commonly used in baking, with white castor sugar being the most commonly used because of its fine grain/texture. Light and dark brown sugars contain molasses and are used to impart additional flavour to baked goods. Icing sugar is powdered sugar with a little corn flour added to it to keep it from clumping together. Substituting the type of sugar called for in a recipe may affect the outcome of the baked good, so always follow the recipe and understand the baking process before making any variations.

LIGHT AND SPONGY

SPONGE CAKES

Easy Sponge Cake 22

Pandan Coconut Sponge Cake 24

Chocolate Sponge Cake 27

Fruit Sponge Flan Cake 28

Orange Sponge Cake 32

Almond Sponge Cake with Buttercream Frosting 35

CHIFFON CAKES

Grapefruit Chiffon Cake 38

Kiwifruit Chiffon Cake 40

Cempedak Chiffon Cake 43

Two-tone Chiffon Cake 44

Macadamia Chiffon Cake 46

Cream Cheese Chiffon Cake 49

Easy Sponge Cake

Makes one 23-cm round cake

Cornflour *80 g*
Self-raising flour *80 g*
Plain (all-purpose) flour *80 g*
Baking powder *1 tsp*
Eggs *4, large, at room temperature*
Castor sugar *240 g*
Vanilla extract *2 tsp*

- Preheat oven to 180°C. Line and grease a 23-cm round cake pan.
- Sift cornflour, self-raising flour, plain flour and baking powder together 3 times to mix and aerate flours. Set aside.
- Using an electric mixer with a whisk attachment, beat eggs at moderately high speed for about 8 minutes until thick and creamy.
- Add sugar by the tablespoonful and beat until sugar dissolves. Takes about 5 minutes or more.
- Add vanilla extract and mix well.
- Transfer egg mixture into a large basin to make it easier to fold in dry ingredients.

NOTE: Use a light hand and a few quick strokes to fold the mixtures together.

Heavy handling of the flours when folding will result in a tough and flat sponge.

- Pour half the sifted flour into egg mixture. Using a metal spatula, lightly fold flour through. Repeat to fold in remaining portion of flour.
- Pour batter into prepared cake pan until about three-quarters full. Smoothen surface of batter with the back of a large metal spoon.
- Bake for about 40 minutes or until a skewer inserted into the centre of cake comes out clean.
- When cake is done, remove from oven. Leave cake in pan for about 5 minutes before unmoulding to cool completely on a wire rack.

Pandan Coconut Sponge Cake

Makes one 20-cm square cake

Self-raising flour *160 g*
Salt *a pinch*
Egg yolks *6, medium, at room temperature*
Corn oil *90 ml*
Pandan paste *1 tsp*
Pandan juice *1 Tbsp (see Note)*
Coconut milk *2 Tbsp*
Fresh milk *2 Tbsp*
Castor sugar *80 g + 80 g*
Egg whites *6, medium, at room temperature*
Cream of tartar *1 tsp*
Icing sugar (optional) *for dusting*

- Preheat oven to 170°C. Line and grease a 20-cm square cake pan.
- Sift flour and salt together 3 times.
- Using an electric mixer with a paddle attachment, cream egg yolks, corn oil, pandan paste, pandan juice, coconut milk, milk, flour mixture and 80 g sugar at medium speed for 2 minutes.
- Using a grease-free mixing bowl and with a whisk attachment, whip egg whites with cream of tartar for 1 minute. Gradually add in remaining sugar and beat for another 2 minutes or until stiff peaks form.
- Using a metal spatula, fold one-third of egg white meringue into egg yolk mixture. Mix well. Fold in rest of egg white meringue gently but quickly.
- Pour batter into prepared cake pan. Bake for 40–45 minutes or until top of cake is brown and a skewer inserted into the centre of cake comes out clean.
- Remove cake from oven and unmould from pan. Leave cake inverted on a wire rack to cool.
- Cake can be served warm, dusted with icing sugar.

NOTE: To obtain pandan juice, blend 3–4 pandan leaves with 1 Tbsp water and strain the juice.

When folding the egg whites into the egg yolk mixture, use a few quick strokes so as not to deflate the egg whites too much. The egg whites give the cake its light texture.

Oven temperatures will vary depending on the size, type and brand of the oven, so the baking times given here need to be adjusted according to how your oven works. To test if a cake is done, insert a skewer into the centre of cake. If the skewer comes out clean, the cake should be done.

Chocolate Sponge Cake

Makes one 23-cm square cake

Cornflour *45 g*

Self-raising flour *150 g*

Unsweetened cocoa powder *2 Tbsp*

Baking powder *1 tsp*

Egg yolks *6, medium, at room temperature*

Castor sugar *120 g + 150 g*

Corn oil *120 ml*

Water *100 ml*

Vanilla extract *2 tsp*

Chocolate emulco *2 tsp*

Egg whites *7, medium, at room temperature*

Cream of tartar *1 tsp*

Chocolate shavings *as needed*

MILK CHOCOLATE ICING (OPTIONAL)

Unsalted butter *100 g*

Unsweetened cocoa powder *2 Tbsp*

Icing sugar *200 g, sifted*

Chocolate milk *4 Tbsp, heated*

Vanilla extract *3 tsp*

- Preheat oven to 170°C. Line and grease a 23-cm square cake pan.
- Sift cornflour, self-raising flour, cocoa powder and baking powder together 3 times. Set aside.
- Using an electric mixer with a paddle attachment, beat egg yolks at medium speed for 2 minutes until thick and pale. Gradually add 120 g sugar and beat well for another 2 minutes at high speed.
- Reduce mixer speed and add flour mixture. Beat for another 2 minutes.
- Add corn oil, water, vanilla extract and chocolate emulco, and continue beating for another 2 minutes. The mixture will be sticky and smooth.
- Using a whisk attachment and a grease-free bowl, whisk egg whites at medium speed for 1 minute, then add cream of tartar and beat for 30 seconds. Gradually add 150 g sugar and whisk at high speed for another 2 minutes until stiff peaks form. Be careful not to overwork the egg whites or it will break down and you will get froth and water.

NOTE: Use metal mixing bowls when baking, as it is easier to get rid of any grease. Washing the mixing bowls with warm water will also help.

Do not over beat the egg yolk mixture. Once the mixture is smooth, stop beating or the resulting sponge will be tough.

- Using a metal spatula, fold half the egg white meringue into egg yolk mixture. When incorporated, continue to fold in the remaining egg white meringue. Do this gently but quickly.
- Pour batter into prepared cake pan and bake for 40–50 minutes until a skewer inserted into the centre of cake comes out clean.
- Remove cake from oven. Leave cake in pan for 10 minutes before unmoulding to cool completely on a wire rack.
- Serve on its own or covered with milk chocolate icing and garnished with chocolate shavings.
- To make milk chocolate icing, melt butter over simmering water or a water bath. Mix in cocoa powder, icing sugar, hot chocolate milk and vanilla extract. Set aside to cool. Using an electric mixer with a paddle attachment, beat mixture until smooth and spreadable.

Fruit Sponge Flan Cake

Makes one 23-cm round cake

Cake flour *100 g*

Cornflour *100 g*

Salt *½ tsp*

Eggs *8, medium, at room temperature*

Castor sugar *240 g*

Vanilla extract *3 tsp*

Extra light virgin olive oil *140 ml*

Selection of fresh fruit

- Preheat oven to 180°C. Line and grease a 23-cm round cake pan.
- Sift cake flour, cornflour and salt together 3 times. Set aside.
- Using an electric mixer with a whisk attachment, whisk eggs and sugar at medium-high speed for about 10 minutes until light and fluffy.
- Add vanilla extract and olive oil and beat for another 2 minutes.
- Using a metal spatula, fold in flour mixture, taking care not to deflate eggs.
- Pour batter into prepared cake pan and bake for 1 hour or until a skewer inserted into the centre of cake comes out clean. The cake will sink slightly in the centre.
- Remove cake from oven. Leave cake in pan for 5 minutes before unmoulding to cool completely on a wire rack. Leave cake to cool inverted.
- Arrange fruit on cake.

NOTE: As an alternative to a cake pan, a flan tin can be used to bake this cake.

Instead of fresh fruit, canned fruit cocktail can be used. Drain canned fruit well before use.

Because of the cornflour used in this recipe, there will be a thin crust that forms on the bottom of the cake. Peel it off together with the greaseproof paper or slice it off with a knife.

The technique to making a good sponge or chiffon cake is in the mixing of the batter. Mix lightly with just a few quick strokes to keep the mixture aerated.

Orange Sponge Cake

Makes one 23-cm round cake

Plain (all-purpose) flour *300 g*
Baking powder *2 Tbsp*
Salt *1 tsp*
Unsalted butter *160 g, softened*
Castor sugar *260 g*
Eggs *3, large, at room temperature*
Oranges *2, grated for zest and squeezed for 160 ml juice*
Orange cloudy emulco *4 tsp*

ORANGE WHIPPED CREAM (OPTIONAL)

Whipping cream *100 ml*
Orange cloudy emulco *1 tsp*

- Line and grease two 23-cm round baking pans. Preheat oven to 170°C.
- Sift flour, baking powder and salt together 3 times.
- Using an electric mixer with a paddle attachment, cream butter and sugar at medium-high speed for 6 minutes.
- Add eggs one at a time and beat for 20 seconds after each addition.
- Add orange zest, then orange juice and mix well.
- Add orange cloudy emulco.
- Add sifted flour mixture into batter and mix until just combined. Scrape down the sides of the mixer at least once and cream for another 20 seconds.

NOTE: Orange zest is the outer rind of the orange that contains the fruit's flavour.

If desired, you can use 5–6 small ramekins in place of baking pans. Reduce the baking time to 20–25 minutes.

- Pour batter equally into the two prepared baking pans.
- Place pans into oven and bake for 30–35 minutes or until top of cakes are golden brown and cakes start to pull away from the sides of pan.
- Leave cakes to cool in pan for 5 minutes before inverting cakes onto a wire rack and removing from pan to cool completely.
- When cool, sandwich the cakes together with orange whipped cream, then cover cake with remaining whipped cream. Decorate cake as desired.
- To make orange whipped cream, use a chilled mixing bowl and whisk. Whip cream for about 3 minutes until glossy, then add orange cloudy emulco and mix well. Keep refrigerated until ready to use.

Almond Sponge Cake with Buttercream Frosting

Makes one 23-cm round cake

Cake flour *160 g*

Baking powder *1 tsp*

Salt *½ tsp*

Eggs *5, large, at room temperature, yolks and whites separated*

Castor sugar *100 g + 100 g*

Corn oil *90 ml*

Cold water *60 ml*

Vanilla extract *1 tsp*

Almond extract *1 tsp*

Ground almonds *200 g*

Cream of tartar *1 tsp*

Toasted whole, sliced or ground almonds *50 g*

BUTTERCREAM FROSTING

Unsalted butter *125 g, softened*

Icing sugar *200 g, sifted*

Warm milk *1 Tbsp*

- Preheat oven to 170°C. Line and grease a 23-cm round cake pan. Set aside.
- Sift flour, baking powder and salt together 3 times. Set aside.
- Using an electric mixer with a whisk attachment, whisk egg yolks and 100 g sugar at medium-high speed for 6–8 minutes until light and fluffy.
- Add corn oil, cold water, vanilla and almond extracts and beat for another 2 minutes.
- Add flour mixture and ground almonds and beat for 2 minutes to form a smooth paste. Set aside.
- Using a whisk attachment and a grease-free bowl, whisk egg whites at medium speed for 1 minute, then add cream of tartar and beat for 30 seconds. Gradually add remaining 100 g sugar and whisk at high speed for another 2–3 minutes until stiff peaks form. Be careful not to overwork the egg whites or it will break down and you will get froth and water.

NOTE: Fold the egg white meringue into the egg yolk mixture in a few big and quick strokes to avoid deflating the batter too much.

- Using a metal spatula, fold half the egg white meringue into egg yolk mixture. When incorporated, continue to fold in the remaining egg white meringue. Do this gently but quickly.
- Pour batter into prepared cake pan until about two-thirds full.
- Bake for about 50 minutes or until the top of cake springs back when gently pressed with a finger.
- Remove cake from oven and leave in pan for 10 minutes before unmoulding to cool completely on a wire rack.
- Meanwhile, prepare buttercream frosting. Using an electric mixer, beat butter, icing sugar and warm milk at low speed until mixture is well blended and smooth. Leave to stand if necessary until frosting is of a spreadable consistency. Chill before using.
- Frost cake with buttercream and garnish with whole, sliced or ground almonds.

To remove a chiffon cake from a tube pan, run a knife around the side of the tube pan and centre core. Remove the cake, then run a knife around the base of the cake. Invert the cake and remove the base.

Grapefruit Chiffon Cake

Makes one 23-cm chiffon cake

Cake flour *300 g*

Baking powder *1 Tbsp*

Salt *1 tsp*

Egg yolks *7, large, at room temperature*

Golden castor sugar *180 g +150 g*

Corn oil *125 ml*

Freshly squeezed grapefruit juice *150 ml, mixed with 40 ml water*

Grapefruit zest *3 Tbsp*

Egg whites *8, large, at room temperature*

Cream of tartar *¾ tsp*

Snow powder or icing sugar *for dusting*

- Preheat oven to 160°C. Prepare a 23-cm tube pan. Do not grease pan.
- Sift flour, baking powder and salt together 3 times.
- Using an electric mixer with a paddle attachment, beat egg yolks at low speed for 1 minute. Gradually add 180 g sugar in a steady stream and beat for about 3 minutes until light and creamy.
- Mix in half the flour mixture and beat for another minute.
- Add corn oil, grapefruit juice and grapefruit zest and continue to beat for 2 minutes.
- Add rest of flour mixture and mix until incorporated. The mixture should be thick and sticky. Set aside.
- Using a whisk attachment and a grease-free bowl, whisk egg whites at medium speed for 1 minute, then add cream of tartar and increase speed to high. Beat for 30 seconds, then gradually add 150 g sugar and whisk for 2–3 minutes until stiff peaks form. The meringue should be firm and glossy, not dry.

NOTE: Do not open the oven door unnecessarily when baking. However, if the top of cake browns too quickly, make a few holes in a sheet of aluminium foil and place over the cake. Do this only after 30 minutes of baking. Remove foil 10 minutes before the cake is done.

All ovens have their own characteristics, so where baking temperature and time is concerned, adjust accordingly. You may have to try the recipe out a few times to get the correct baking temperature and time.

- Using a metal spatula, fold half the egg white meringue into egg yolk mixture. When incorporated, continue to fold in the remaining egg white meringue. Do this gently but quickly.
- Pour batter into the ungreased tube pan. Gently tap the pan on a hard surface to release any air bubbles. Smoothen the surface of the batter with the back of a metal spoon.
- Place tube pan on the bottom shelf of the oven and bake for 20 minutes. Lower the temperature to 150°C and bake for another 25 minutes. Lower the temperature a second time to 140°C and bake for a further 30 minutes. A skewer inserted into the centre of cake should come out clean.
- Remove cake from oven and immediately invert pan. Let cake cool completely in inverted pan before removing. Takes about 2 hours.
- To remove cake from pan, run a knife around the side of tube pan and centre core, then around the base.
- Place cake upright on a serving plate. Dust with snow powder or icing sugar before slicing to serve.

Kiwifruit Chiffon Cake

Makes one 23-cm chiffon cake

Cake flour *280 g*

Baking powder *1 ½ tsp*

Salt *¾ tsp*

Egg yolks *6, medium, at room temperature*

Egg *1, at room temperature*

Egg whites *7, medium, at room temperature*

Castor sugar *140 g + 100 g*

Corn oil *120 ml*

Kiwifruit *1, peeled and blended to get about 80 g purée*

Freshly squeezed orange juice *1 Tbsp*

Rose water *2 tsp*

Cream of tartar *½ tsp*

VANILLA ICING (OPTIONAL)

Skimmed or fresh milk *150 ml*

Plain (all-purpose) flour *4 Tbsp, sifted*

Unsalted butter *150 g, softened*

Icing sugar *100–150 g, sifted*

Vanilla extract *2 tsp*

- Preheat oven to 170°C. Prepare a 23-cm tube pan. Do not grease pan.
- Sift flour, baking powder and salt together 3 times.
- Using an electric mixer with a paddle attachment, beat 6 egg yolks and 1 whole egg at low speed for 1 minute. Gradually add 140 g sugar in a steady stream and beat for another 1 minute until light and creamy.
- Add corn oil, kiwifruit purée, orange juice and rose water and continue to beat for 2 minutes to blend well.
- Add flour mixture and mix until incorporated. Takes about 1 minute. The mixture should be thick. Scrape down the sides of the bowl. Set aside.
- Using a whisk attachment and a grease-free bowl, whisk 7 egg whites at medium speed for 1 minute, then add cream of tartar and increase speed to high. Beat for 30 seconds, then gradually add 100 g sugar and whisk for 3–4 minutes until stiff peaks form. The meringue should be firm and glossy, not dry.
- Using a metal spatula, fold half the egg white meringue into egg yolk mixture. When incorporated, continue to fold in the remaining egg white meringue. Do this gently but quickly.

NOTE: Using 80 g kiwifruit purée is just right for this cake, as using more will weigh down the cake and cause it to sink.

- Pour batter into the ungreased tube pan. Gently tap the pan on a hard surface to release any air bubbles. Smoothen the surface of the batter with the back of a metal spoon.
- Place tube pan at the bottom shelf of the oven and bake for 20 minutes. Lower the temperature to 160°C and bake for another 45 minutes or until cake is golden brown and springy to the touch. Cover the top of the cake with aluminium foil if the cake browns too quickly after 30 minutes of baking.
- Remove cake from oven and immediately invert pan. Let cake cool completely in inverted pan before removing. Takes about 2 hours.
- To remove cake from pan, run a knife around the side of tube pan and centre core, then around the base.
- Serve cake on its own or topped with vanilla icing.
- To make vanilla icing, combine 150 ml milk and sifted flour in a small saucepan. Cook over low heat for about 4 minutes, stirring often with a whisk until mixture is thick and resembles soft whipped cream. Set aside to cool slightly. Using an electric mixer with a paddle attachment, beat butter, icing sugar and vanilla extract at medium speed for about 5 minutes until smooth. Gradually add cooled milk mixture and beat until icing is smooth, creamy and of a spreadable consistency. Add more milk or icing sugar to adjust the consistency if necessary.

Cempedak Chiffon Cake

Makes one 23-cm chiffon cake

Cake flour *260 g*

Baking powder *1½ tsp*

Salt *½ tsp*

Egg yolks *7, medium, at room temperature*

Golden castor sugar *140 g +120 g*

Corn oil *120 ml*

Very ripe cempedak *5–6 pieces, blended to get 100 g purée*

Water *2 Tbsp*

Rose water *2 tsp*

Egg whites *8, medium, at room temperature*

Cream of tartar *1 tsp*

- Preheat oven to 170°C. Prepare a 23-cm tube pan. Do not grease pan.
- Sift flour, baking powder and salt together 3 times.
- Using an electric mixer with a paddle attachment, beat egg yolks, 140 g sugar, corn oil, cempedak purée, water, rose water and flour mixture together at medium speed for about 4 minutes until smooth. Set aside.
- Using a whisk attachment and a grease-free bowl, whisk egg whites at medium speed for 1 minute, then add cream of tartar and increase speed to high. Beat for 30 seconds, then gradually add 120 g sugar and whisk for 3–4 minutes until stiff peaks form. The meringue should be firm and glossy, not dry.
- Using a metal spatula, fold half the egg white meringue into egg yolk mixture. When incorporated, continue to fold in the remaining egg white meringue. Do this gently but quickly.

NOTE: Rose water is very aromatic and can be used as a flavour enhancer when baking cakes.

- Pour batter into the ungreased tube pan. Gently tap the pan on a hard surface to release any air bubbles. Smoothen the surface of the batter with the back of a metal spoon.
- Place tube pan at the bottom shelf of the oven and bake for 30 minutes. Lower the temperature to 150°C and bake for another 40 minutes or until cake is golden brown and springy to the touch. Cover the top of the cake with aluminium foil if the cake browns too quickly after 30 minutes of baking.
- Remove cake from oven and immediately invert pan. Let cake cool completely in inverted pan before removing. Takes about 2 hours.
- To remove cake from pan, run a knife around the side of tube pan and centre core, then around the base. Allow cake to sit for a day before serving. This cake will keep for up to 3 days at room temperature.

Two-tone Chiffon Cake

Makes one 23-cm chiffon cake

Cake flour 200 g
Baking powder 1½ tsp
Salt ¼ tsp
Golden castor sugar 125 g + 125 g
Eggs 8, medium, at room temperature, yolks and whites separated
Unsalted butter 250 g, melted and cooled
Sweetened condensed milk 3 Tbsp
Vanilla extract 2 tsp
Cocoa powder 2 tsp
Chocolate emulco 2 tsp
Hot water 2 Tbsp
Cream of tartar ½ tsp

- Preheat oven to 170°C. Prepare a 23-cm tube pan. Do not grease pan.
- Sift flour, baking powder and salt together 3 times. Stir in 125 g sugar and make a well in the centre.
- Mix egg yolks, butter, condensed milk and vanilla extract and pour into the centre of flour and sugar mixture.
- Using an electric mixer with a paddle attachment, beat mixture at medium speed for 5–6 minutes until a smooth but sticky mixture is obtained.
- Meanwhile, mix cocoa powder, chocolate emulco and hot water together.
- Scoop out half the egg yolk mixture and set aside. Add cocoa powder and chocolate emulco mixture to remaining egg yolk mixture and blend well using the electric mixer. Set aside.
- Using a whisk attachment and a grease-free bowl, whisk egg whites at medium speed for 1 minute, then add cream of tartar and increase speed to high. Beat for 30 seconds, then gradually add 125 g sugar and whisk for 3 minutes until stiff peaks form. The meringue should be firm and glossy, not dry.

NOTE: When folding the egg white meringue into the egg yolk mixture, use a gentle hand and do it in 2 batches, with about 15 turns each time. This prevents the beaten egg whites from deflating during folding.

- Using a metal spatula, fold half the egg white meringue lightly into the plain egg yolk mixture. Fold the other half of the egg white meringue lightly into the cocoa batter. Do not worry if there are white streaks.
- Scoop out half the plain batter into a small bowl. Do the same with the cocoa batter, then pour both batters into the ungreased tube pan at the same time, so half the pan is filled with plain batter and the other half is filled with cocoa batter. Repeat with the remaining plain and cocoa batter, but this time, pour the cocoa batter over the side with the plain batter.
- Place tube pan at the bottom shelf of the oven and bake for 20 minutes. Lower the temperature to 150°C and bake for another 40–45 minutes or until cake is golden brown and springy to the touch. Cover the top of the cake with aluminium foil if the cake browns too quickly after 30 minutes of baking.
- Remove cake from oven and immediately invert pan. Let cake cool completely in inverted pan before removing. Takes about 2 hours.
- To remove cake from pan, run a knife around the side of tube pan and centre core, then around the base.

Macadamia Chiffon Cake

Makes one 23-cm chiffon cake

Cake flour *225 g*

Baking powder *1½ tsp*

Salt *½ tsp*

Egg yolks *7, medium, at room temperature*

Castor sugar *130 g + 130 g*

Corn oil *140 ml*

Fresh milk *50 ml*

Freshly squeezed orange juice *1 Tbsp*

Rose water *2 tsp*

Vanilla extract *2 tsp*

Roasted macadamia nuts *100 g, ground; reserve 2 Tbsp*

Egg whites *8, medium, at room temperature*

Cream of tartar *½ tsp*

GANACHE (OPTIONAL)

Whipping cream *250 ml*

Baking chocolate (70% cocoa) *150 g, coarsely chopped*

Rum or brandy (optional) *2 Tbsp*

- Preheat oven to 170°C. Prepare a 23-cm tube pan. Do not grease pan.
- Sift flour, baking powder and salt together 3 times.
- Using an electric mixer with a paddle attachment, beat flour mixture, egg yolks, 130 g sugar, corn oil, milk, orange juice, rose water, vanilla extract and ground macadamia nuts at medium speed for about 4 minutes until smooth and sticky. Set aside.
- Using a whisk attachment and a grease-free bowl, whisk egg whites at medium speed for 1 minute, then add cream of tartar and increase speed to high. Beat for 30 seconds, then gradually add 130 g sugar and whisk for 3–4 minutes until stiff peaks form. The meringue should be firm and glossy, not dry.
- Using a metal spatula, fold half the egg white meringue into egg yolk mixture. When incorporated, continue to fold in the remaining egg white meringue. Do this gently but quickly.
- Pour half the batter into the ungreased tube pan, then sprinkle over the reserved 2 Tbsp ground macadamia nuts. Pour in the rest of the batter. Gently tap the pan on a hard surface to release any air bubbles. Smoothen the surface of the batter with the back of a metal spoon.

NOTE: To roast your own macadamia nuts, preheat the oven to 160°C and roast for 10 minutes. The macadamia nuts in this recipe can be substituted with other nuts like hazelnuts and walnuts.

- Place tube pan at the bottom shelf of the oven and bake for 25 minutes. Lower the temperature to 150°C and bake for another 40 minutes or until cake is golden brown and springy to the touch. Cover the top of the cake with aluminium foil if the cake browns too quickly after 30 minutes of baking.
- Remove cake from oven and immediately invert pan. Let cake cool completely in inverted pan before removing. Takes about 2 hours.
- To remove cake from pan, run a knife around the side of tube pan and centre core, then around the base.
- Serve cake on its own or topped with chocolate ganache.
- To prepare chocolate ganache, bring whipping cream to a boil in a heavy-based saucepan over medium-high heat. Pour hot whipping cream over baking chocolate and stir with a hand-held whisk until smooth. Add rum or brandy, if desired.

Cream Cheese Chiffon Cake

Makes one 23-cm chiffon cake

Cream cheese 125 g, softened
Unsalted butter 4 Tbsp
Castor sugar 80 g + 80 g
Cake flour 80 g, sifted
Fresh milk 100 ml, mixed with 4 Tbsp cornflour
Egg yolks 5, medium, at room temperature
Vanilla extract 3 tsp
Freshly squeezed lemon juice 1 Tbsp
Lemon zest 1 tsp
Egg whites 6, medium, at room temperature
Cream of tartar 1 tsp

ORANGE BUTTERCREAM ICING (OPTIONAL)

Unsalted butter 150 g, at room temperature
Icing sugar 100 g + 200 g, sifted
Freshly squeezed orange juice 2 Tbsp
Orange paste 2 tsp
Rose water 1 tsp

- Preheat oven to 180°C. Prepare a 23-cm tube pan. Do not grease pan.
- Using an electric mixer with a paddle attachment, beat cream cheese, butter and 80 g sugar at medium speed for 1 minute.
- Add flour, milk mixture, egg yolks, vanilla extract, lemon juice and lemon zest and continue to beat for another 2 minutes until mixture is thick. Set aside.
- Using a whisk attachment and a grease-free bowl, whisk egg whites at medium speed for 1 minute, then add cream of tartar and increase speed to high. Beat for 30 seconds, then gradually add 80 g sugar and whisk for 3–4 minutes until stiff peaks form. The meringue should be firm and glossy, not dry.
- Using a metal spatula, fold half the egg white meringue into egg yolk mixture. When incorporated, continue to fold in the remaining egg white meringue. Do this gently but quickly.
- Pour batter into the ungreased tube pan, then gently tap the tube pan on a hard surface to release any air bubbles. Using the back of a metal spoon, smoothen the surface of the batter.

NOTE: This cake is lightly flavoured with cream cheese. If you prefer a stronger flavour, increase the quantity of cream cheese to 150 g.

- Place tube pan at the bottom shelf of the oven and bake for 20 minutes. Lower the temperature to 160°C and bake for another 1 hour 5 minutes or until cake is golden brown and springy to the touch.
- Remove cake from oven and immediately invert pan. Let cake cool completely in inverted pan before removing. Takes about 2 hours.
- To remove cake from pan, run a knife around the side of tube pan and centre core, then around the base. Allow cake to sit for a day before serving. This cake will keep for up to 3 days at room temperature.
- Serve on its own or covered with orange buttercream icing. This cake tastes great chilled.
- To make orange buttercream icing, use an electric mixer with a paddle attachment and beat together butter, 100 g icing sugar and orange juice at medium speed for about 6 minutes until smooth and creamy. Gradually add remaining 200 g icing sugar and continue to beat until very smooth. Add orange paste and rose water and beat for another 2 minutes.

SITTING PRETTY

CUPCAKES

Avocado Cupcakes with Chocolate Frosting 52

Orange Cupcakes with Butter Icing 55

Pine Nut and Star Fruit Cupcakes with
Honey Cream Cheese Frosting 58

Mini Kopi-O Cupcakes with Coffee Buttercream Icing 60

Chocolate Cupcakes with Chocolate Frosting 65

Pandan Chiffon Cupcakes with Coconut Frosting 66

MUFFINS

Pistachio Muffins 68

Buttermilk-Milo Muffins 71

Savoury Cheesy Muffins 72

White Chocolate Chilli Muffins 76

Triple Chocolate Cherry Muffins 79

Banana and Blueberry Muffins 80

Avocado Cupcakes with Chocolate Frosting

Makes 9–12 cupcakes

Plain (all-purpose) flour *280 g*

Baking powder *2 tsp*

Bicarbonate of soda *1 tsp*

Salt *1 tsp*

Very ripe avocado *¾, medium, pitted and peeled*

Soy milk *100 ml*

Unsalted butter *225 g, at room temperature*

Light brown sugar *90 g*

Eggs *3, large, at room temperature*

Vanilla extract *2 tsp*

Rose water *2 tsp*

CHOCOLATE FROSTING (OPTIONAL)

Dark chocolate *75 g*

Unsalted butter *125 g, softened*

Icing sugar *130 g, sifted*

Vanilla extract *1 tsp*

Chocolate milk *7 tsp*

- Preheat oven to 180°C. Line a cupcake tray with 9–12 paper cases.
- Sift flour, baking powder, bicarbonate of soda and salt together 3 times into a large mixing bowl. Set aside.
- Purée avocado with soy milk in a food processor until smooth and creamy.
- Using an electric mixer and with a paddle attachment at medium speed, cream butter and sugar for about 3 minutes.
- Add eggs one at a time and beat for about 20 seconds after each addition.
- Add one-third of the flour mixture into the butter mixture and mix well. Add half the avocado mixture and beat for 30 seconds. Add half the remaining flour mixture and mix well. Add the rest of the avocado mixture and beat for another 30 seconds. Add the rest of the flour mixture and mix to combine. You should have a smooth batter.

NOTE: These cupcakes will shrink slightly after baking.

Cupcakes with frosting can be kept for up to 3 days in an airtight container in the refrigerator. Leave at room temperature for at least 30 minutes before serving.

- Spoon batter into prepared paper cases until about three-quarters full. Bake for about 30 minutes or until a skewer inserted into the centre of cakes comes out clean.
- Remove from oven and allow cupcakes to cool completely on a wire rack.
- To make chocolate frosting, melt chocolate in a bowl set over simmering water. Stir well, then remove from heat. Beat butter with an electric mixer at high speed for 2 minutes. Reduce speed to low, add icing sugar and continue beating for another 2 minutes. Scrape down the sides of the mixing bowl and beat for another 2 minutes on high until smooth.
- Add melted chocolate and vanilla extract and beat for 1 minute. Slowly add in chocolate milk until a spreadable consistency is obtained. Turn mixer to high speed and beat for a further 30 seconds. Chill frosting for about 20 minutes before using.
- Spoon chocolate frosting into a piping bag fitted with a piping tip and decorate cupcakes as desired. Serve immediately.

Orange Cupcakes with Butter Icing

Makes 9–12 cupcakes

Self-raising flour *120 g*
Salt *a pinch*
Unsalted butter *125 g, softened*
Golden castor sugar *120 g*
Eggs *2, medium, at room temperature*
Orange zest *1 tsp*
Vanilla extract *1 tsp*
Freshly squeezed orange juice *3 Tbsp*

BUTTER ICING

Unsalted butter *80 g, softened*
Icing sugar *130 g, sifted*
Chilled fresh milk *1 Tbsp*

- Preheat oven to 190°C. Line a cupcake tray with 9–12 paper cases.
- Sift flour and salt together 3 times into a large mixing bowl.
- Using an electric mixer with a paddle attachment at medium-high speed, beat butter and sugar for 6 minutes until light in colour and creamy.
- Add eggs one at a time and beat for 20 seconds after each addition. Add orange zest and vanilla extract and beat for another 20 seconds.
- Remove bowl from mixer and using a metal spatula, fold in flour in 3 additions.
- Add orange juice to combine and to give it a soft dropping consistency.

NOTE: To add some colour to the butter icing, replace the milk with freshly squeezed orange juice and a few drops of orange cloudy emulco.

- Using a dessert spoon, scoop batter into prepared paper cases until just slightly over half-full.
- Bake for about 35 minutes until golden brown or until a skewer inserted into the centre of cakes comes out clean.
- Remove from oven and leave on a wire rack to cool completely.
- To serve, pipe butter icing on cupcakes and decorate as desired.
- To make butter icing, cream butter with icing sugar using an electric mixer with a paddle attachment at medium speed. Beat for about 6 minutes until mixture is light in colour. Add milk and continue to beat for another 2 minutes.

Decorating cupcakes is one of my favourite things to do! Just whip up a frosting and get creative!

Pine Nut and Star Fruit Cupcakes with Honey Cream Cheese Frosting

Makes 9–12 cupcakes

Cake flour *150 g*

Plain (all-purpose) flour *150 g*

Baking powder *2 tsp*

Bicarbonate of soda *½ tsp*

Salt *½ tsp*

Ripe star fruit *1–2, sliced, seeds removed + a few slices for garnishing*

Rose water *3 tsp*

Unsalted butter *250 g, softened*

Golden castor sugar *100 g*

Light brown sugar *100 g*

Eggs *4, large, at room temperature*

Pine nuts *150 g, toasted in a 160°C oven for 10 minutes*

HONEY CREAM CHEESE FROSTING

Unsalted butter *150 g, softened*

Cream cheese *150 g, softened*

Orange zest *3 tsp*

Honey *1 tsp*

Freshly squeezed orange juice *2 Tbsp*

Vanilla extract *1 tsp*

Icing sugar *200 g, sifted*

- Preheat oven to 180°C. Line a cupcake tray with 9–12 paper cases.

- Sift cake flour, plain flour, baking powder, bicarbonate of soda and salt together 3 times into a large mixing bowl. Set aside.

- Purée star fruit and rose water in a blender until smooth. Measure out 100 ml purée. Set aside.

- Using an electric mixer with a paddle attachment at medium speed, beat butter for 2 minutes until soft. Gradually add sugars and beat for another 3 minutes.

- Change mixer speed to low. Add eggs one at a time and beat for 20 seconds after each addition.

- Add half the flour mixture into the butter mixture and beat for 30 seconds.

- Spoon in puréed star fruit mixture and mix well.

- Add rest of flour mixture and beat well for 1 minute until incorporated. Add pine nuts to combine.

NOTE: Rose water enhances the flavour of the cupcakes. Substitute with vanilla extract, if desired.

When choosing fruit for baking, always select ripe fruit.

- Spoon batter into prepared paper cups, filling them to the brim. Cupcakes will sink slightly after baking.

- Bake for 25–30 minutes or until a skewer inserted into the centre of cakes comes out clean.

- Remove from oven and leave to cool on a wire rack for 15 minutes before frosting.

- Using a piping bag with a star nozzle, pipe honey cream cheese frosting on cupcakes and decorate with a slice of star fruit.

- To make frosting, cream butter and cream cheese together using an electric mixer with a paddle attachment and at medium-high speed for about 5 minutes, until light and fluffy. Add orange zest, honey, orange juice and vanilla extract and mix for 30 seconds. Add icing sugar a spoonful at a time until a spreading consistency is obtained. Refrigerate for about 20 minutes to chill before using.

Mini Kopi-O Cupcakes with Coffee Buttercream Icing

Makes about 28 mini cupcakes

Dark chocolate *60 g, chopped*
Self-raising flour *100 g*
Plain (all-purpose) flour *100 g*
Baking powder *1 tsp*
Salt *½ tsp*
Ground almonds (optional) *20 g*
Local brewed coffee without sugar (kopi-o) *100 ml*
Baileys Irish Cream or any coffee liqueur *2 Tbsp*
Unsalted butter *150 g, softened*
Castor sugar *60 g*
Light brown sugar *60 g*
Eggs *2, large, at room temperature*
Vanilla extract *1 tsp*

COFFEE BUTTERCREAM ICING

Dark chocolate *100 g, chopped*
Whipping cream *100 ml*
Instant coffee granules *1½ Tbsp*
Unsalted butter *125 g, softened*
Icing sugar *150 g, sifted*

- Preheat oven to 170°C. Line a mini cupcake tray with about 28 paper cases.
- Place chopped dark chocolate in a microwave-safe bowl and heat in the microwave oven for 30 seconds on High. Remove and stir chocolate, then return to microwave oven and heat for another 30 seconds until completely melted.
- In a large bowl, sift self-raising flour, plain flour, baking powder and salt together 3 times. Add ground almonds, if using, and mix well. Set aside.
- Mix coffee with Irish cream or coffee liqueur. Set aside.
- Using an electric mixer with a paddle attachment, beat butter and sugars at medium-high for 8 minutes until pale and creamy.
- Add eggs one at a time and beat for 20 seconds after each addition. Add vanilla extract.
- Reduce mixer speed to low and add one-third of flour mixture to combine. Pour in half of the coffee mixture and beat well. Add half of the remaining flour mixture and beat to combine. Pour in remaining coffee mixture and mix, then add rest of flour mixture. Beat for another 1 minute.
- Add melted chocolate and mix well.
- Spoon batter into paper cases.
- Bake for 15–20 minutes until cupcakes are firm to the touch.
- Remove from oven and allow to cool completely on a wire rack.
- Once cooled, pipe with coffee buttercream icing and decorate with a chocolate coated coffee bean if desired.
- To make coffee buttercream icing, melt dark chocolate with whipping cream over simmering water in a double boiler. Stir in instant coffee granules. Set aside to cool. With an electric mixer, beat butter, 100 g icing sugar and cooled chocolate mixture together at medium-high speed for about 6 minutes until smooth. Gradually add remaining icing sugar until a creamy texture of spreading consistency is achieved. Add more icing sugar if necessary. Refrigerate icing for 20 minutes before using.

NOTE: *Kopi-o*, a local hand-brewed coffee, can be purchased from local coffee shops.

From the pretty paper cases to the wide range of frostings, these bite-size treats always make me smile!

Chocolate Cupcakes with Chocolate Frosting

Makes 9–12 cupcakes

Self-raising flour *180 g*

Unsweetened cocoa powder *100 g*

Bicarbonate of soda *½ tsp*

Salt *½ tsp*

Unsalted butter *200 g, softened*

Castor sugar *200 g*

Eggs *2, large, at room temperature*

Vanilla extract *2 tsp*

Chocolate milk *180 ml*

Freshly squeezed orange juice *2 Tbsp*

Milk or dark chocolate chips *150 g*

CHOCOLATE FROSTING

Unsalted butter *130 g, softened*

Dark chocolate *130 g*

Whipping or light cream *80 ml*

Icing sugar *150 g, sifted*

- Preheat oven to 160°C. Line a cupcake tray with 9–12 paper cases or place 9–12 paper cups on a baking tray.

- In a large bowl, sift flour, cocoa powder, bicarbonate of soda and salt together 3 times. Set aside.

- Using an electric mixer with a paddle attachment, beat butter and sugar for 6 minutes at medium-high speed until light and fluffy.

- Add eggs one at a time and beat for 20 seconds after each addition. Add vanilla extract, chocolate milk and orange juice and beat until combined. Takes about 1 minute.

- Reduce mixer speed to low and add flour mixture. Beat until incorporated.

- Carefully, spoon batter into prepared paper cases, filling each half-full. Add a few chocolate chips and top with remaining batter until three-quarters full.

NOTE: If desired, replace the chocolate milk in this recipe with plain fresh milk.

As a variation to this recipe, you can use any type of chocolate. Just chop into pieces before using.

- Bake for about 25 minutes until tops of cakes are golden brown or a skewer inserted into the centre of cakes comes out clean.

- Remove from oven and allow to cool completely on a wire rack.

- Once cooled, ice cupcakes with chocolate frosting and serve immediately.

- To make frosting, combine unsalted butter, dark chocolate and cream together in a medium saucepan over medium heat. Stir with a wooden spoon until smooth. Remove from heat and stir in icing sugar. Using an electric mixer with a whisk attachment, whisk mixture at medium-high speed until frosting is of the right spreading consistency. Keep aside for about 1 hour to set before using.

Pandan Chiffon Cupcakes with Coconut Frosting

Makes 9–12 cupcakes

Cake flour *125 g*

Baking powder *1 tsp*

Pandan leaves *20*

Egg yolks *6, medium, at room temperature*

Corn oil *120 ml*

Freshly squeezed coconut milk *110 ml*

Castor sugar *60 g + 120 g*

Egg whites *7, medium, at room temperature*

Salt *1 tsp*

COCONUT FROSTING

Unsalted butter *80 g, softened*

Cream cheese *80 g, softened*

Icing sugar *80 g, sifted*

Cream of coconut *3 Tbsp (see Note)*

Rum (optional) *1 tsp*

Desiccated coconut *80 g*

- Preheat oven to 160°C. Line a cupcake tray with 9–12 paper cases or place 9–12 paper cups on a baking tray.
- In a large bowl, sift flour and baking powder 3 times. Set aside.
- Wash pandan leaves, then chop into small pieces. Place into a blender with about 3 Tbsp water and blend well. Strain the blended mixture to obtain 5–6 Tbsp pandan juice.
- Using an electric mixer with a paddle attachment, mix flour mixture, egg yolks, corn oil, coconut milk, pandan juice and 60 g sugar at medium-high speed for about 3 minutes until smooth.
- Using a whisk attachment and a grease-free bowl, whisk egg whites for 1 minute, then add salt and whisk for another few seconds until frothy. Slowly and gradually add 120 g sugar and whisk for another 2–3 minutes until stiff peaks form. The meringue should be firm and glossy, not dry.

NOTE: Cream of coconut is not the same as coconut milk. It is available in packets from supermarkets.

- Stir half the meringue into the egg yolk mixture and mix until combined. Use a metal spatula and with a light hand, fold in the rest of the meringue until thoroughly mixed.
- Spoon the batter into the prepared cupcake moulds until three-quarters full.
- Place on the lowest rack of the oven and bake for 20–25 minutes until top of cupcakes are golden brown and a skewer inserted into the centre of cakes comes out clean.
- Remove from oven and allow to cool completely on a wire rack. The cupcakes will sink slightly.
- Decorate cupcakes with coconut frosting before serving.
- To make frosting, beat butter and cream cheese until smooth. Reduce speed to low and add icing sugar, cream of coconut and rum. Mix to combine. Increase mixer speed to high, then add desiccated coconut and beat until light and fluffy. Takes about 6 minutes.

Pistachio Muffins

Makes about 9 muffins

Plain (all-purpose) flour *250 g*

Double-action baking powder *2 tsp*

Salt *a pinch*

Granulated sugar *180 g*

Unsalted pistachio nuts *120 g, coarsely chopped*

Eggs *2, medium, at room temperature*

Fresh milk *160 ml*

Unsalted butter *100 g, melted*

- Preheat oven to 200°C. Grease or line a 9-hole muffin pan.
- Sift flour, baking powder and salt together 3 times. Add sugar and chopped pistachios. Mix well. Make a well in the centre and set aside.
- In another bowl, beat eggs until slightly foamy, then add milk, followed by melted butter. Mix well.
- Pour egg mixture into flour mixture, stirring with a wooden spoon until just combined. The batter should be slightly lumpy.
- Spoon batter into prepared muffin pan, filling each cup up to three-quarters full.
- Bake for 20–25 minutes or until a skewer inserted into the centre of muffins comes out clean.
- Remove from oven. Leave muffins in pan for about 10 minutes before removing to a wire rack to cool.

NOTE: To decorate these muffins, use whipped cream and chopped pistachios. Whisk about 100 ml whipping cream for 3–4 minutes until soft peaks form. Spoon into a piping bag and pipe rosettes on each muffin. Sprinkle with ground pistachios.

Vary this recipe by replacing the pistachios with other nuts such as pine nuts and walnuts.

Buttermilk-Milo Muffins

Makes about 12 muffins

Plain (all-purpose) flour *250 g*
Baking powder *2 tsp*
Salt *½ tsp*
Granulated sugar *120 g*
Milo powder *75 g + 75 g*
Eggs *2, medium, at room temperature*
Corn oil *100 ml*
Buttermilk *250 ml*
Light sour cream *2 Tbsp*
Freshly squeezed orange juice *2 Tbsp*
Orange zest *1 tsp*

ORANGE ICING
Icing sugar *100 g, sifted*
Butter *30 g, melted*
Freshly squeezed orange juice *3 tsp*

- Preheat oven to 200°C. Grease or line a 12-hole muffin pan.
- Sift flour, baking powder and salt together 3 times. Add sugar and 75 g Milo powder. Mix well. Make a well in the centre and set aside.
- In another bowl, beat together eggs, corn oil, buttermilk, sour cream, orange juice and orange zest.
- Pour egg mixture into flour mixture, stirring with a wooden spoon until just combined. The batter should be slightly lumpy.

NOTE: As a variation to this recipe, replace the Milo powder with instant coffee granules to make coffee muffins.

- Spoon batter into prepared muffin pan, filling each cup up halfway. Spoon and sprinkle 1 tsp Milo powder into the centre of each cup, then continue to spoon more batter over until cups are three-quarters full.
- Bake for 20–25 minutes or until a skewer inserted into the centre of muffins comes out clean.
- Remove from oven. Leave muffins in pan for about 10 minutes before removing to a wire rack to cool. Serve warm on its own or covered with orange icing.
- To make orange icing, whisk icing sugar, butter and orange juice together for 2 minutes. Spoon into a piping bag and pipe onto muffins.

Savoury Cheesy Muffins

Makes about 12 muffins

Cream cheese 100 g, softened
Castor sugar 2 Tbsp + 125 g
Freshly squeezed lemon juice 1 Tbsp
Vanilla extract 1 tsp
Plain (all-purpose) flour 250 g
Baking powder 2 tsp
Salt ½ tsp
Lemon zest 1 tsp
Paprika 1 tsp
Corn oil 125 ml
Fresh milk 150 ml
Light sour cream 2 Tbsp
Eggs 2, large, at room temperature
Cheddar cheese 60 g, cubed

- Preheat oven to 200°C. Grease or line a 12-hole muffin pan.
- Using an electric mixer and with a paddle attachment, beat cream cheese with 2 Tbsp castor sugar at medium speed for 2 minutes. Add lemon juice and vanilla extract and beat for another minute. Set aside.
- In a separate bowl, sift flour, baking powder and salt together 3 times. Add 125 g castor sugar, lemon zest and paprika. Mix to combine. Make a well in the centre and set aside.
- In another bowl, whisk together corn oil, milk, sour cream and eggs.
- Pour egg mixture into flour mixture, stirring with a wooden spoon until just combined. The batter should be slightly lumpy.

NOTE: Savoury muffins are best eaten on the day of baking. They do not store well.

- Spoon batter into prepared muffin pan, filling each cup up halfway. Drop 1 tsp cream cheese mixture and 1–2 cubes cheddar cheese into each cup, then spoon a little more batter over to cover. Do not add too much batter as it might overflow while baking. Keep the cups just slightly over half-full.
- Place muffins on the lowest rack of the oven and bake for about 30 minutes.
- Remove from oven. Leave muffins in pan for about 10 minutes before removing to a wire rack to cool. Serve warm.

Unlike cupcakes, muffins have a fuller texture and I love how you can just mix the ingredients together without needing a mixer.

White Chocolate Chilli Muffins

Makes about 12 muffins

Plain (all-purpose) flour *250 g*

Double-action baking powder *2 tsp*

Salt *½ tsp*

Castor sugar *150 g*

White chocolate chips *150 g*

Chilli flakes *2½ Tbsp*

White chocolate *100 g, chopped*

Fresh milk *250 ml*

Eggs *2, large, at room temperature*

Corn oil *150 ml*

Vanilla extract *2 tsp*

Rose water *1 tsp*

- Preheat oven to 200°C. Grease or line a 12-hole muffin pan.
- Sift flour, baking powder and salt together 3 times. Add sugar, white chocolate chips and chilli flakes and mix well. Make a well in the centre and set aside.
- Place chopped white chocolate in a microwave-safe bowl and heat in the microwave oven for 30 seconds on High. Remove and stir chocolate, then return to microwave oven and heat for another 30 seconds until completely melted.
- In another bowl, whisk together milk, eggs, corn oil, vanilla extract, rose water and melted white chocolate.
- Pour egg mixture into flour mixture, stirring with a wooden spoon until just combined. The batter should be slightly lumpy.
- Spoon batter into muffin pan, filling each cup three-quarters full.
- Bake for 20–25 minutes or until muffins are golden brown and firm to the touch.
- Remove from oven. Leave muffins in pan for about 10 minutes before removing to a wire rack to cool.
- Serve warm, with more chilli flakes sprinkled over the top if desired.

NOTE: If you would like an even spicier muffin, remove the seeds of 1–2 red chillies and dice. Add to the flour mixture.

To make dark chocolate chilli muffins, replace the white chocolate chips with dark chocolate chips and the melted white chocolate with 2 Tbsp cocoa powder sifted with the flour mixture.

Triple Chocolate Cherry Muffins

Makes about 12 muffins

Plain (all-purpose) flour 250 g + 1 Tbsp
Unsweetened cocoa powder 3 Tbsp
Baking powder 2 tsp
Bicarbonate of soda 1 tsp
Salt ½ tsp
Golden castor sugar 80 g
Soft light brown sugar 80 g
Dark chocolate chips 100 g + more for topping
Canned pitted cherries 1 can (439 g), drained
Unsweetened chocolate 100 g, chopped
Eggs 2, large, at room temperature
Sunflower oil 185 ml
Chocolate milk 200 ml
Honey 1 tsp
Vanilla extract 2 tsp

CHOCOLATE FUDGE FROSTING

Unsalted butter 125 g, cut into cubes
Unsweetened chocolate 125 g, chopped
Whipping cream 125 ml

- Preheat oven to 200°C. Grease or line a 12-hole muffin pan.
- Sift 250 g flour, cocoa powder, baking powder, bicarbonate of soda and salt together 3 times. Stir in sugars and chocolate chips. Mix well. Make a well in the centre and set aside.
- Sprinkle 1 Tbsp flour over drained cherries to coat lightly.
- Place chopped chocolate in a microwave-safe bowl and heat in the microwave oven for 30 seconds on High. Remove and stir chocolate, then return to microwave oven and heat for another 30 seconds until completely melted.
- In a big bowl, whisk together eggs, sunflower oil, chocolate milk, melted chocolate, honey and vanilla extract until mixture is thoroughly combined.
- Pour egg mixture into flour mixture, stirring with a wooden spoon until just combined. The batter should be slightly lumpy.

NOTE: As a variation to this recipe, use white chocolate chips in place of dark chocolate chips.

- Spoon 2 Tbsp batter into each muffin cup, then press 1–2 pitted cherries into batter. Spoon more batter over until cups are three-quarters full. Top each muffin with 3–4 chocolate chips, if desired.
- Bake for 25–30 minutes or until a skewer inserted into the centre of muffins comes out clean.
- Remove from oven. Leave muffins in pan for about 10 minutes before removing to a wire rack to cool.
- Serve muffins warm on their own or topped with chocolate fudge frosting.
- To make chocolate fudge frosting, melt butter and chocolate in a bowl set over simmering water. Mix well, then remove from heat. Stir in whipping cream and leave to cool for 20 minutes. Whisk cooled mixture for 2 minutes or until thickened to a spreadable consistency.
- Without frosting, the muffins will keep for up to 3 days at room temperature or up to a week in the freezer. Reheat in the oven before serving if frozen.

Banana and Blueberry Muffins

Makes about 12 muffins

Plain (all-purpose) flour *260 g*
Baking powder *2½ tsp*
Bicarbonate of soda *½ tsp*
Salt *½ tsp*
Castor sugar *180 g*
Dried blueberries *200 g*
Ripe bananas *2, medium*
Sour cream *60 ml*
Buttermilk *120 ml*

Eggs *2, large, at room temperature*
Unsalted butter *180 g, melted*
Lemon zest *2 tsp*
Orange zest *1 tsp*
Vanilla extract *1 tsp*
Fresh blueberries *for garnishing*

CINNAMON-SUGAR
Icing sugar *80 g, sifted*
Ground cinnamon *3 tsp*

- Preheat oven to 200°C. Grease or line a 12-hole muffin pan.
- Sift flour, baking powder, bicarbonate of soda and salt together 3 times. Add sugar and dried blueberries. Mix thoroughly and make a well in the centre. Set aside.
- Purée bananas, sour cream and buttermilk using a blender until smooth.
- In another bowl, beat together eggs, melted butter, puréed banana mixture, lemon zest, orange zest and vanilla extract. Set aside.
- Pour egg mixture into flour mixture, stirring with a wooden spoon until just combined. The batter will be lumpy.

NOTE: When making muffins, stir the liquid mixture into the flour mixture only until just moistened for a light texture. Do not use an electric mixer to beat the mixture or the muffins will have a coarse texture.

Dried blueberries can be substituted with fresh or frozen blueberries.

Give the muffins an extra crunch by sprinkling demerara sugar over the top of the muffins before baking.

- Using a metal spoon, scoop the batter into the prepared muffin pan, filling each cup three-quarters full. Press 2–3 fresh blueberries on top of each muffin.
- Place the pan on the bottom shelf of the oven and bake for 20–25 minutes or until golden brown or a skewer inserted into the centre of muffins comes out clean.
- Remove muffins from the oven and let cool in pan for about 10 minutes. Remove muffins from pan and let cool on a wire rack completely.
- If desired, top the muffins with cinnamon-sugar. Mix icing sugar with ground cinnamon and place on a flat plate. When muffins are cooled, brush tops with cold melted butter, then roll in cinnamon-sugar. Serve.

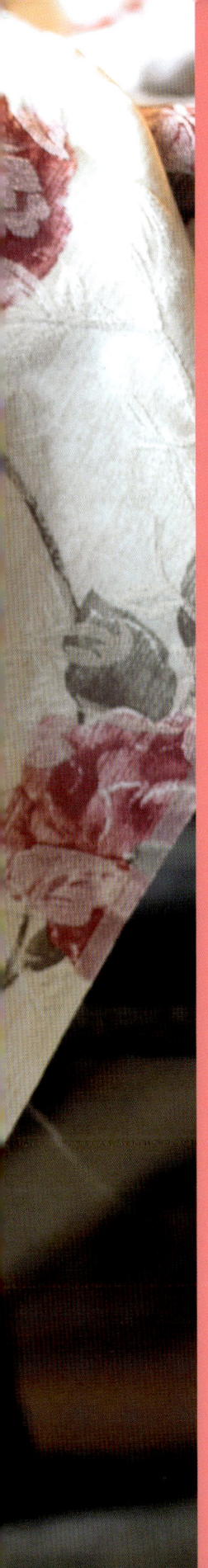

OLD FASHION-NO NONSENSE

LOAF CAKES

Butter Loaf *84*

Banana Loaf *86*

Your Choice Loaf *88*

Candied Ginger Loaf *90*

Chocolate Loaf *92*

Hazelnut Loaf *94*

CHOCOLATE CAKES

Simple Chocolate Cake *98*

Chocolaty Chocolate Cake *100*

Glam Chocolate Cake *104*

Your Date Chocolate Cake *106*

Fudgy Chocolate Cake *109*

FRUIT CAKES

Almond Fruit Cake *110*

Red Wine Fruit Cake *112*

Hi-5 Fruit Cake *115*

Easy Fruit Cake *116*

English Fruit Cake *118*

White Chocolate Fruit Cake *121*

Butter Loaf

Makes two 19 x 9-cm loaves

Unsalted butter 250 g, at room temperature
Castor sugar 250 g
Self-raising flour 200 g
Eggs 7, medium, at room temperature
Fresh milk 1 Tbsp, chilled
Freshly squeezed orange juice 1 Tbsp, chilled
Vanilla extract ¾ Tbsp

- Preheat oven to 180°C. Line and grease two 19 x 9-cm loaf pans.
- Chill butter and sugar for 10 minutes before using.
- Sift self-raising flour 3 times.
- Using an electric mixer and with a paddle attachment at medium speed, cream butter and sugar for about 15 minutes.
- Add eggs one at a time and beat for 30 seconds after each addition.

NOTE: To make marble loaves, divide the batter into 3 parts. Add 1 Tbsp chocolate emulco to one part and mix well. Set aside. Divide a portion of the plain batter equally into the prepared pans, then spoon the chocolate batter in dollops onto it. Cover with the remaining portion of plain batter and use a chopstick to swirl the batter to create a marble effect. Bake as above.

- Add milk, orange juice and vanilla extract and beat for another 30 seconds until combined.
- With the mixer at low speed, add flour a little at a time and beat until mixture is smooth. Time it in such a way that all the flour will be mixed in 2 minutes.
- Divide the batter into the prepared loaf pans and bake for 45 minutes or until a skewer inserted into the centre of cakes comes out clean.
- Leave cakes in pans for 20 minutes before removing to a wire rack to cool completely before serving.

Banana Loaf

Makes two 19 x 9-cm loaves

Plain (all-purpose) flour *250 g*
Double-action baking powder *1 tsp*
Bicarbonate of soda *1 tsp*
Salt *½ tsp*
Unsalted butter *250 g, softened*
Golden castor sugar *250 g*

Eggs *5, medium, at room temperature*
Very ripe bananas *5–6, peeled and mashed*
Banana extract *½ tsp*
Vanilla extract *1 tsp*
Fresh milk *6 Tbsp*

- Preheat oven to 160°C. Line and grease two 19 x 9-cm loaf pans.
- Sift flour, baking powder, bicarbonate of soda and salt together 3 times. Set aside.
- Using an electric mixer with a paddle attachment, cream butter and sugar at medium-high speed until light and fluffy. Takes about 5 minutes. Scrape down the sides and bottom of the bowl.
- Add eggs one at a time and beat for 20 seconds after each addition. Add mashed bananas, banana extract and vanilla extract and beat until incorporated. Takes about 1 minute.

NOTE: Do not over mix the batter or the texture of cake will be hard.

As a variation to this recipe, add 1 Tbsp honey and ½ tsp ground cinnamon to the batter. Add together with the mashed bananas.

- Change mixer speed to low and gradually add flour mixture. Mix well. Add milk to achieve a smooth batter.
- Pour batter into prepared pans and bake for about 45 minutes or until a skewer inserted into the centre of cakes comes out clean.
- Remove from oven. Leave cake to cool in pan for 5 minutes before removing to cool completely on a wire rack.

Your Choice Loaf

Makes one 22 x 13-cm loaf

Plain (all-purpose) flour *275 g*

Double-action baking powder *1 tsp*

Bicarbonate of soda *1 tsp*

Salt *½ tsp*

Unsalted butter *275 g, softened*

Castor sugar *275 g*

Eggs *4, large, at room temperature*

Vanilla extract *2 tsp*

Butter oil *1 tsp (see Note)*

Rose water *2 tsp*

Your choice of carbonated drink *150 ml*

- Preheat oven to 160°C. Line and grease a 22 x 13-cm loaf pan.
- Sift flour, baking powder, bicarbonate of soda and salt together 3 times. Set aside.
- Using an electric mixer with a paddle attachment, cream butter at medium-high speed for about 6 minutes, then add sugar in a steady stream. Mix well to combine. Scrape down the sides of the bowl.
- Add eggs one at a time and beat for 20 seconds after each addition. Add vanilla extract, butter oil and rose water and continue beating for 30 seconds.
- Change mixer speed to low and add one-third of flour mixture until just incorporated, followed by half of the drink. Add half the remaining flour mixture and mix well. Add the rest of the drink, followed by the rest of the flour mixture, mixing to combine after each addition.
- Pour batter into prepared pan and bake for about 1 hour or until a skewer inserted into the centre of cake comes out clean.
- Remove from oven. Leave cake to cool in pan for 5 minutes before removing to cool completely on a wire rack.

NOTE: Butter oil is a flavouring and can be purchased from the baking section of supermarkets and baking specialty stores.

Candied Ginger Loaf

Makes one 22 x 13-cm loaf

Plain (all-purpose) flour 250 g

Double-action baking powder 1 tsp

Bicarbonate of soda ¼ tsp

Unsalted butter 250 g, softened

Golden castor sugar 150 g

Eggs 4, medium, at room temperature

Egg yolk 1, medium, at room temperature

Golden syrup 2 Tbsp

Vanilla extract 2 tsp

Blueberry syrup (from canned blueberries) 150 ml

Candied ginger 180 g, finely chopped

LEMON BUTTERCREAM ICING

Unsalted butter 125 g, softened

Freshly squeezed lemon juice 2 Tbsp

Lemon zest 2 tsp

Lemon paste 2 tsp

Icing sugar 350 g, sifted

- Preheat oven to 160°C. Line and grease a 22 x 13-cm loaf pan.
- Sift flour, baking powder and bicarbonate of soda together 3 times.
- Using an electric mixer with a paddle attachment, beat butter and sugar until light and fluffy. Takes about 8 minutes.
- Add eggs and egg yolk one at a time and beat for 20 seconds after each addition. Add golden syrup and vanilla extract and mix well.

NOTE: As a variation to this recipe, replace blueberry syrup with fresh milk.

- Change mixer speed to low and add one-third of flour mixture until just combined, followed by half the blueberry syrup. Add half the remaining flour mixture and mix well. Add the rest of the blueberry syrup, followed by the rest of the flour mixture, mixing to combine after each addition.
- Add candied ginger and mix well.
- Spoon batter into prepared loaf pan and bake for about 1 hour or until a skewer inserted into the centre of cake comes out clean.
- Remove from oven. Leave cake to cool in pan for 5 minutes before removing to cool completely on a wire rack. Serve warm on its own or topped with lemon buttercream icing.
- To make lemon buttercream icing, beat butter, lemon juice, zest and paste and icing sugar together for 8–10 minutes until smooth and creamy.

Chocolate Loaf

Makes one 25.5 x 11.5-cm loaf

Plain (all-purpose) flour *150 g*
Double-action baking powder *1 tsp*
Bicarbonate of soda *½ tsp*
Salt *½ tsp*
Unsweetened cocoa powder *4 Tbsp*
Evaporated milk *120 ml, warmed*
Unsalted butter *125 g, softened*
Golden castor sugar *125 g*
Eggs *3, medium, at room temperature*
Vanilla extract *1 Tbsp*

CHOCOLATE ICING
Unsweetened chocolate *100 g*
Unsalted butter *50 g*
Icing sugar *50 g, sifted*
Fresh milk *2 Tbsp*

- Preheat oven to 180°C. Line and grease a 25.5 x 11.5-cm loaf pan.
- Sift flour, baking powder, bicarbonate of soda and salt together 3 times. Set aside.
- Combine cocoa powder and warm evaporated milk. Stir well and let cool.
- Using an electric mixer with a paddle attachment, cream butter and sugar at medium-high speed until light and fluffy. Takes about 6 minutes. Scrape down the sides of the bowl.
- Add eggs one at a time and beat for 20 seconds after each addition. Add vanilla extract to mix.
- Change mixer speed to medium and add one-third of flour mixture until just combined, followed by half of the milk mixture. Add half the remaining flour mixture and mix well. Add the rest of the milk mixture, followed by the rest of the flour mixture, mixing to combine after each addition.

NOTE: This cake requires a long baking time. Covering it with aluminium foil 30 minutes into the baking time prevents the top of the cake from over-browning.

- Pour batter into prepared pan and bake for about 30 minutes.
- Make some holes in a sheet of aluminium foil large enough to cover top of cake. Place aluminium foil over cake, then continue to bake for another 30 minutes. Remove foil and bake for another 5 minutes.
- Remove from oven. Leave cake to cool in pan for 5 minutes before removing to cool completely on a wire rack.
- Spread cake with chocolate icing or dust with a mixture of unsweetened cocoa powder and icing sugar, if desired before serving.
- To make icing, stir chocolate and butter in a double boiler or bowl set over simmering water until melted and smooth. Stir in icing sugar and milk. Whisk well and let stand for about 1 hour before spreading on cake.

Hazelnut Loaf

Makes one 22 x 13-cm loaf

Self-raising flour *170 g*
Baking powder *½ tsp*
Salt *½ tsp*
Unsalted butter *125 g, softened*
Castor sugar *125 g*
Eggs *2, large, at room temperature*
Vanilla extract *1 tsp*
Chocolate milk *4 Tbsp*
Unsweetened cocoa powder
 2 Tbsp, mixed with 3 Tbsp hot water
Chocolate hazelnut spread *3 Tbsp*
Hazelnuts *100 g, toasted and ground*

- Preheat oven to 180°C. Line and grease a 22 x 13-cm loaf pan.
- Sift flour, baking powder and salt together 3 times. Set aside.
- Using an electric mixer with a paddle attachment, beat butter and sugar at medium-high speed until light and fluffy. Takes about 6 minutes. Scrape down the sides of the bowl.
- Add eggs one at a time and beat for 20 seconds after each addition. Add vanilla extract and beat until incorporated. Takes about 30 seconds.
- Change mixer speed to low and add one-third of flour mixture until just combined, followed by half of the milk. Add half the remaining flour mixture and mix well. Add the rest of the milk, followed by the rest of the flour mixture, mixing to combine after each addition.

NOTE: This cake can be stored in an airtight container in a cool place for up to 3 days.

As a variation to this recipe, replace hazelnuts with other nuts such as pine nuts or almonds and omit the hazelnut spread.

- Set one-third of batter aside.
- Add cocoa mixture, chocolate hazelnut spread and ground hazelnuts to remaining batter and mix well.
- Pour half the hazelnut batter into prepared pan, top with reserved plain batter and cover with remaining portion of hazelnut batter. Using a chopstick, swirl the batter to create a marble effect. Bake for about 15 minutes.
- Make some holes in a sheet of aluminium foil large enough to cover top of cake. Place aluminium foil over cake, lower oven temperature to 160°C, then continue to bake for another 25 minutes. Remove foil and bake for another 10 minutes.
- Remove from oven. Leave cake to cool in pan for 5 minutes before removing to cool completely on a wire rack.

Loaf cakes, chocolate cakes and fruit cakes are hearty, wholesome cakes that never fail to satisfy my sweet cravings.

Simple Chocolate Cake

Makes one 23-cm round cake

Cake flour *70 g*

Salt *a pinch*

Unsweetened chocolate (70% cocoa) *300 g, chopped*

Unsalted butter *200 g, cut into cubes*

Eggs *6, large, at room temperature, yolks and whites separated*

Castor sugar *200 g*

Chocolate rice *80 g, mixed with 1 Tbsp cake flour*

Cream of tartar *½ tsp*

Icing sugar or snow powder *as needed*

- Preheat oven to 180°C. Line and grease a 23-cm round cake pan.
- Sift flour and salt together 3 times. Set aside.
- Melt chocolate using a double boiler over medium heat or in a bowl set over simmering water. Add butter and stir to mix. Set aside.
- Using an electric mixer with a paddle attachment, beat egg yolks with sugar at medium-high speed for about 5 minutes until pale and creamy.
- Pour melted chocolate and butter mixture into egg yolk mixture and beat for another 1 minute.
- Reduce speed to low and add in sifted flour by the spoonful. Add chocolate rice.
- Using a clean, grease-free bowl, whisk egg whites with cream of tartar until stiff peaks form. Takes about 3 minutes.
- Fold egg white meringue in 2 portions into egg yolk mixture. Do this gently and quickly.
- Pour batter into prepared cake pan and bake for 55 minutes or until a skewer inserted into the centre of cake comes out clean.
- Remove from oven and leave cake to cool in pan for 15 minutes. Remove cake from pan and allow to cool completely on a wire rack. Sprinkle top of cake with icing sugar or snow powder, if desired.

NOTE: Do not open the oven door unnecessarily when baking. However, if the top of cake browns too quickly, make a few holes in a sheet of aluminium foil and place over cake. Do this only after 30 minutes of baking or as instructed in the recipe. Remove foil 10 minutes before cake is done.

Chocolaty Chocolate Cake

Makes one 23-cm square cake

Self-raising flour *350 g*

Bicarbonate of soda *1 tsp*

Salt *¼ tsp*

Bitter chocolate (70% cocoa) *250 g, chopped*

Unsalted butter *250 g, softened*

Dark brown sugar *250 g*

Vanilla extract *2 tsp*

Eggs *4, medium, at room temperature*

Buttermilk *250 ml*

Boiling water *125 ml, mixed together with 3 Tbsp cocoa powder*

Chocolate chips *160 g, coated with 1 Tbsp self-raising flour*

Chocolate-coated hazelnuts *as needed*

FROSTING (OPTIONAL)

Bitter chocolate (70% cocoa) *125 g, chopped*

Cream cheese *500 g, softened*

Unsalted butter *125 g, cut into cubes*

Bottled caramel fudge sauce *250 ml, reserve 2–3 Tbsp for decorating cake*

- Preheat oven to 180°C. Line and grease a 23-cm square cake pan.
- Sift flour, bicarbonate of soda and salt together 3 times. Set aside.
- Melt chocolate using a double boiler over medium heat or in a bowl set over simmering water. Set aside.
- Using an electric mixer with a paddle attachment, cream butter and sugar at medium-high speed for about 5 minutes until soft and creamy.
- Add vanilla extract and beat for 30 seconds.
- Add eggs one at a time and beat for 20 seconds after each addition.
- Change mixer speed to low and add in one-third of flour mixture until incorporated, followed by half of the buttermilk. Add half the remaining flour mixture and mix well. Add the rest of the buttermilk, followed by the rest of the flour mixture, mixing to combine after each addition.
- Beat in melted chocolate and cocoa mixture. The mixture should be thin. Fold in chocolate chips.

NOTE: Coating the chocolate chips with flour prevents them from sinking to the bottom of the cake while baking.

- Pour batter into prepared cake pan and bake for 30 minutes. Lower oven temperature to 160°C and bake for another 30 minutes or until a skewer inserted into the centre of cake comes out clean except where it might have touched some chocolate chips.
- Remove cake from oven and leave to cool in pan for 15 minutes. Remove cake from pan and allow to cool completely on a wire rack.
- Prepare frosting, if desired. Melt chocolate in a double boiler over medium heat or in a bowl set over simmering water. Set aside. Using an electric mixer with a paddle attachment, beat cream cheese and butter at medium-high speed for about 5 minutes until soft. Gradually add in melted chocolate and caramel fudge sauce and beat until well mixed. Refrigerate to chill before using.
- Meanwhile, using a serrated knife, slice a thin layer off the top of cooled cake and discard. Cut cake into 2 or 3 layers. Working quickly, spread frosting between layers of cake, then over top and sides of cake.
- Drizzle reserved caramel fudge sauce over top of cake and use a metal skewer to swirl the caramel into the frosting to create a marble effect. Garnish with chocolate-coated hazelnuts, if desired.

Glam Chocolate Cake

Makes one 23-cm round cake

Plain (all-purpose) flour *280 g*

Unsweetened cocoa powder *70 g*

Baking powder *1 tsp*

Bicarbonate of soda *1 tsp*

Salt *½ tsp*

Unsalted butter *420 g*

Castor sugar *310 g + 110 g*

Eggs *7, large, , at room temperature, yolks and whites separated*

Vanilla extract *2 tsp*

Brandy *2 Tbsp*

Chocolate milk *5 Tbsp*

WHITE CHOCOLATE FROSTING

Unsalted butter *250 g, cut into cubes*

Whipping cream *200 ml*

White chocolate buttons *150 g*

White chocolate *150 g, chopped*

SYRUP

Water *180 ml*

Castor sugar *90 g*

Cointreau or freshly squeezed orange juice *4 Tbsp*

- Prepare white chocolate frosting. Using a double boiler or a bowl set over simmering water, melt ingredients for frosting over medium heat. Stir occasionally until mixture is smooth. Remove from heat and leave to cool to room temperature. Cover with plastic wrap and chill for 1 hour. Beat white chocolate frosting at medium speed for about 6 minutes or until pale and creamy. Refrigerate frosting until needed.

- Preheat oven to 170°C. Line and grease a 23-cm round cake pan.

- Sift flour, cocoa powder, baking powder, bicarbonate of soda and salt together 3 times. Set aside.

- Using an electric mixer with a paddle attachment, cream butter and 310 g sugar at medium-high speed for about 10 minutes. Add egg yolks one at a time and beat for 20 seconds after each addition. Add vanilla extract and brandy and mix thoroughly. Add chocolate milk.

- Using a clean, grease-free bowl, whisk egg whites at medium speed for 1 minute. Add 110 g sugar gradually and whisk for about 2 minutes until stiff peaks form.

- Fold half the egg white meringue into the egg yolk mixture until well-mixed, then add the rest of egg white meringue and mix thoroughly. Do this quickly.

- Fold in flour mixture in 3 additions with quick, big strokes using a metal spatula.

- Pour batter into prepared cake pan and bake for about 1 hour or until a skewer inserted into the centre of cake comes out clean.

- Remove cake from oven and leave to cool in pan for 10 minutes. Remove cake from pan and leave to cool completely on a wire rack.

- Cut a thin layer off the top of cooled cake and discard. Slice cake into 2 layers.

- Prepare syrup. Boil water with sugar over medium heat, stirring until sugar dissolves. Stir in Cointreau or orange juice. Brush syrup over cake.

- Working quickly, spread frosting between layers of cake, then over top of cake. Decorate cake with fruit of choice.

NOTE: The cake will sink slightly after baking.

If using canned fruit to decorate cake, drain well in a sieve, then dab dry with kitchen towels before using. If using fresh fruit, wash well before using.

As a variation to this recipe, replace the white chocolate with dark chocolate.

Your Date Chocolate Cake

Makes one 23-cm round cake

Pitted prunes 200 g, chopped
Dates 150 g, chopped
Dark rum 6 Tbsp
Cashew nuts 100 g
Self-raising flour 150 g
Unsweetened cocoa powder 150 g
Baking powder ½ tsp
Bicarbonate of soda 1 tsp
Salt ½ tsp
Plain milk chocolate 300 g
Unsalted butter 200 g, softened
Castor sugar 200 g
Eggs 5, large, at room temperature
Vanilla extract 2 tsp
Chocolate milk 4 Tbsp

ESPRESSO GLAZE (OPTIONAL)

Unsalted butter 2 Tbsp, softened
Unsweetened chocolate 90 g, chopped
Espresso granules 3 Tbsp, dissolved in 6 Tbsp warm water
Icing sugar 200 g, sifted
Vanilla extract 2 tsp

- Soak prunes and dates in rum overnight.
- Preheat oven to 160°C and roast cashew nuts for 10 minutes. Leave to cool before chopping.
- Increase oven heat to 180°C. Line, grease and flour a 23-cm round cake pan.
- Sift flour, cocoa powder, baking powder, bicarbonate of soda and salt together 3 times. Set aside.
- Melt chocolate in a double boiler or in a bowl set over simmering water. Set aside.
- Using an electric mixer with a paddle attachment, cream butter and sugar at medium speed for about 6 minutes until pale and creamy.
- Add eggs one at a time and beat for 30 seconds after each addition.
- Add melted chocolate to incorporate. Add vanilla extract.
- Add one-third of flour mixture and mix until incorporated, followed by half of the milk. Add half the remaining flour mixture and mix well. Add the rest of the milk, followed by the rest of the flour mixture, mixing to combine after each addition.
- Stir in chopped cashew nuts, soaked prunes and dates. Mix well.
- Spoon batter into prepared cake pan and bake for 40–50 minutes or until a skewer inserted into the centre of cake comes out clean.
- Remove from oven and leave to cool in pan for 10 minutes. Remove cake from pan and leave to cool completely on a wire rack.
- Slice and serve as it is or drizzle with espresso glaze.
- To make espresso glaze, stir butter, unsweetened chocolate and espresso in a double boiler over medium heat or a bowl set over simmering water until mixture is glossy. Leave to cool for 5 minutes. Pour cooled mixture into a mixing bowl. Gradually add icing sugar and vanilla extract and whisk until smooth and blended. Use glaze immediately.

Fudgy Chocolate Cake

Makes one 23-cm round cake

Plain (all-purpose) flour *200 g*
Unsweetened cocoa powder *50 g*
Double-action baking powder *1 tsp*
Bicarbonate of soda *1 tsp*
Salt *½ tsp*
Bitter chocolate (70% cocoa) *150 g, chopped*
Unsalted butter *150 g*
Eggs *4, large, at room temperature*
Castor sugar *200 g*
Vanilla extract *2 tsp*
Buttermilk *4 Tbsp*

FUDGE FROSTING

Bitter chocolate (70% cocoa) *250 g, chopped*
Unsalted butter *125 g, cut into cubes*
Whipping cream *170 ml*
Vanilla extract *1 tsp*
Icing sugar *180 g, sifted*

SYRUP

Water *180 ml*
Castor sugar *90 g*

DECORATION

Cocoa powder *as needed, sifted*
Chocolate flakes *as needed*

- Prepare frosting a few hours ahead. Place chocolate and butter in a double boiler or bowl set over simmering water until chocolate melts. Stir in whipping cream. Whisk chocolate mixture with vanilla extract and icing sugar until thick and smooth. Leave to set at room temperature. Do not refrigerate frosting.

- Preheat oven to 170°C. Line and grease a 23-cm round cake pan.

- Sift flour, cocoa powder, baking powder, bicarbonate of soda and salt together 3 times. Set aside.

- Melt chocolate in a double boiler or bowl set over simmering water. Add butter and stir until smooth. Set aside.

- Using an electric mixer with a whisk attachment, whisk eggs, sugar and vanilla extract until mixture is doubled in volume and thickened. Stir in chocolate mixture until incorporated.

NOTE: This cake can be kept refrigerated for up to 3 days. Bring to room temperature or slice, then heat lightly in the microwave oven before serving.

- Change mixer speed to low and add in one-third of flour mixture until incorporated, followed by half of the buttermilk. Add half the remaining flour mixture and mix well. Add the rest of the buttermilk, followed by the rest of the flour mixture, mixing to combine after each addition.

- Pour batter into prepared pan and bake for about 55 minutes or until a skewer inserted into the centre of cake comes out clean. Leave cake in pan for 10 minutes. Turn cake out onto a wire rack and let cool completely.

- Prepare syrup. Boil water and sugar over medium heat, stirring until sugar dissolves.

- Cut a thin layer off the top of cooled cake and discard. Slice cake into 2 layers.

- Brush syrup over cake, then spread some frosting between layers. Cover top and sides of cake with remaining frosting.

- Dust top of the cake with cocoa powder and sprinkle chocolate flakes over. Slice and serve.

Almond Fruit Cake

Makes two 25 x 10-cm loaves or one 23-cm round cake

Brandy *4 Tbsp*
Freshly squeezed orange juice *4 Tbsp*
Plain (all-purpose) flour *200 g*
Baking powder *½ Tbsp*
Unsalted butter *250 g*
Castor sugar *150 g*
Eggs *3, large, at room temperature*
Honey *1 Tbsp*
Vanilla extract *3 tsp*
Chopped almonds *180 g*
Ground almonds *180 g*

DRIED FRUIT

Red glacé cherries *100 g (about 16 pieces), quartered*
Green glacé cherries *100 g (about 16 pieces), quartered*
Dried apricots *180 g, diced*
Dried figs *180 g, diced*
Raisins *120 g*
Sultanas *120 g*
Pitted prunes *180 g, diced*

- Soak red and green glacé cherries in warm water, then rinse with cold water and pat dry.
- Combine brandy and orange juice and soak dried fruit in this mixture overnight.
- Sift flour and baking powder together 3 times.
- Preheat oven to 150°C. Line two 25 x 10-cm loaf pans or a 23-cm round cake pan, leaving a 3-cm overhang all around. Grease lined pan.
- Using an electric mixer with a paddle attachment, cream butter and sugar at medium speed for 7 minutes or until creamy.
- Add eggs one at a time and beat for about 20 seconds after each addition. Add honey and vanilla extract and beat until combined.
- Reduce speed to low, and add flour in 3 additions, reserving 3 Tbsp to coat soaked fruit.
- Fold in chopped and ground almonds, reserving 2 Tbsp chopped almonds.
- Dust soaked fruit with reserved flour. Fold into batter.
- Pour batter into prepared pan. Top with reserved chopped almonds.
- Place cake pan on the lowest rack of the oven and bake for about 1 hour 30 minutes. Reduce oven temperature to 130°C and bake for another 1 hour. If top of cake browns too quickly, make holes in a sheet of aluminium foil and place over cake. Test if cake is done by inserting a skewer into the centre of cake. The skewer should come out clean.
- Remove from oven. Leave cake to cool in pan for 1 hour before removing to cool completely on a wire rack.
- Peel greaseproof paper from cake and wrap with aluminium foil to keep it moist.

NOTE: This cake can be stored at room temperature for up to 2 weeks. To keep the cake moist, turn the cake over and use a skewer to make holes all over the base of cake. Drizzle 1–2 Tbsp brandy on cake every other day.

When lining the pan with greaseproof paper, leaving an overhang not only allows the cake to be removed easily from the pan, but also prevents the cake from browning too much.

Red Wine Fruit Cake

Makes one 23-cm round cake

Hazelnuts *150 g, chopped*
Dark raisins *100 g*
Golden raisins *100 g*
Candied ginger *100 g*
Red wine *100 ml + 3 Tbsp*
Self-raising flour *250 g*
Mixed spice *2 tsp*
Ground ginger *1 tsp*
Unsalted butter *180 g, softened*
Light brown sugar *180 g*
Eggs *3, large, at room temperature*
Maple syrup *½ Tbsp*
Semi-sweet milk chocolate buttons *120 g*

- Soak hazelnuts, raisins and candied ginger together in 100 ml red wine for at least 2 hours, or overnight if time permits.
- Preheat oven to 150°C. Line a 23-cm round cake pan with greaseproof paper, leaving a 3-cm overhang all around. Grease lined pan.
- Sift flour, mixed spice and ground ginger together 3 times.
- Using an electric mixer with a paddle attachment, cream butter and sugar at medium-high speed until light and fluffy. Takes about 8 minutes.
- Add eggs one at a time and beat for 20 seconds after each addition. Mix in maple syrup.
- Change mixer to low speed. Add flour mixture in 3 additions and mix until incorporated.
- Mix in soaked nut and fruit mixture and milk chocolate buttons.
- Pour batter into prepared cake pan and bake for 2 hours 30 minutes or until a skewer inserted into the centre of cake comes out clean.
- Remove from oven. Leave cake to cool completely in pan placed on a wire rack.
- When cool, remove cake from pan. Turn cake over and remove greaseproof paper. Make holes all over cake using a skewer. Sprinkle 3 Tbsp red wine over cake. Wrap cake with a layer of clean greaseproof paper, followed by aluminium foil to keep it moist.
- Cake is best consumed only after 5 days.

NOTE: Instead of baking a whole cake, you can also bake the batter in paper cups. Bake them for 30 minutes until a skewer inserted into the centre of cakes comes out clean.

Hi-5 Fruit Cake

Makes three 25 x 10-cm loaves or two 23-cm round cakes

Mixed dried fruit *1 kg*

Freshly squeezed orange juice *500 ml*

Self-raising flour *500 g*

Canned pineapples *500 g, drained and crushed*

Bottled caramel fudge sauce *120 ml*

Liquor of choice (sherry, rum, brandy) *as needed*

- Soaked mixed dried fruit in orange juice overnight.
- Sift flour 3 times.
- Preheat oven to 130°C. Line three 25 x 10-cm loaf pans or two 23-cm round cake pans, leaving a 3-cm overhang all around. Grease lined pans.
- In a mixing bowl, combine flour with mixed dried fruit and incorporate well. Add crushed pineapples and mix evenly. Add caramel fudge sauce and mix well. Pour batter into cake pans and bake for 2 hours 30 minutes.

NOTE: Bottled caramel fudge sauce can be purchased from most leading supermarkets.

- Remove from oven. Leave cakes to cool completely in pan placed on a wire rack.
- When cool, remove cakes from pans. Turn cakes over and peel off greaseproof paper. Use a skewer to make holes all over cakes. Sprinkle liquor over cakes and do this every other day. Wrap cakes with clean greaseproof paper, followed by aluminium foil to keep them moist.
- Stored in a cool, damp place, this fruit cake will keep for several weeks.

Easy Fruit Cake

Makes one 23-cm round cake

Mixed dried fruit 1 kg
Grapefruit juice with pulp 500 ml
Grapefruit zest 1 Tbsp
Plain (all-purpose) flour 250 g
Double-action baking powder 1 tsp
Ground cinnamon 1 tsp
Mixed spice 1 tsp
Unsalted butter 250 g, softened
Dark muscovado sugar 200 g
Eggs 6, medium, at room temperature
Treacle (optional) 3 Tbsp
Walnuts 200 g, ground
Rum as needed

- Combine mixed dried fruit, grapefruit juice and zest and leave to soak overnight.
- Preheat oven to 140°C. Grease and line a 23-cm round cake pan, leaving a 3-cm overhang all around.
- Sift flour, baking powder, ground cinnamon and mixed spice together 3 times.
- Using an electric mixer with a paddle attachment, cream butter and sugar at medium speed for 10 minutes until light and fluffy. Add eggs one at a time and beat for 30 seconds after each addition. Mix in treacle, if using.
- Remove mixing bowl from mixer. Using a metal spatula, fold in sifted flour mixture by the spoonful.
- Fold mixed dried fruit into batter until incorporated. Repeat to fold in walnuts.
- Pour batter into prepared cake pan and place on the lowest rack of the oven. Bake for about 3 hours or until a skewer inserted into the centre of cake comes out clean.
- When cool, remove cake from pan. Turn cake over and peel off greaseproof paper. Make holes all over cake using a skewer. Drizzle 4 Tbsp rum over cake and repeat every other day. Wrap cake with clean greaseproof paper, followed by aluminium foil to keep it moist.
- Cake is best consumed only after 5 days. Dust with ground cinnamon if desired before serving.

NOTE: To prevent the dried fruit from sinking to the bottom of cake while baking, mix 2 Tbsp flour into the soaked fruit before incorporating into batter.

To make a fruit cake that is chock-full of fruit and nuts easier to slice, refrigerate it for a few hours before slicing.

English Fruit Cake

Makes a 23-cm square cake

Raisins *250 g*

Pitted prunes *250 g, chopped*

Brandy *90 ml + 45 ml + more for drizzling over cake*

Glacé red cherries *50 g*

Glacé green cherries *50 g*

Self-raising flour *150 g*

Baking powder *½ tsp*

Salt *¼ tsp*

Mixed spice *½ Tbsp*

Ground nutmeg *½ tsp*

Ground cinnamon *½ tsp*

Ground cloves *¼ tsp*

Ground ginger *¼ tsp*

Unsalted butter *150 g, softened*

Dark brown sugar *75 g*

Eggs *4, large, at room temperature*

Mixed nuts (walnuts, hazelnuts, macadamia etc.) *50 g, chopped*

Ground almonds *50 g*

- Soak raisins, prunes and cherries in 90 ml brandy overnight.
- Soak glacé cherries in warm water, then rinse with cold water and pat dry.
- Preheat oven to 150°C. Grease and line a 23-cm square cake pan, leaving a 3-cm overhang all around.
- Sift flour, baking powder, salt and all the spices together 3 times.
- Using an electric mixer with a paddle attachment, cream butter and sugar at medium-high speed for about 8 minutes until light and fluffy. Add eggs one at a time and beat for 20 seconds after each addition.
- At low speed, beat in flour mixture in 3 additions until incorporated.
- Add soaked fruit, chopped mixed nuts and ground almonds, followed by 45 ml brandy. Batter should be soft and moist. Add another beaten egg or a little milk to achieve a soft and moist batter, if necessary.
- Pour batter into prepared cake pan and bake for 1 hour, then lower oven temperature to 130°C and bake for a further 2 hours or until a skewer inserted into the centre of cake comes out clean. Remove from oven and leave cake to cool completely in pan placed on a wire rack.
- When cool, remove cake from pan. Turn cake over and peel off greaseproof paper. Make holes all over cake using a skewer. Drizzle 1 Tbsp brandy over cake and repeat every other day. Wrap cake with clean greaseproof paper, followed by aluminium foil to keep it moist.
- Cake is best consumed only after a few weeks.

NOTE: Do not consume this cake immediately after baking as it will be hard and dry. It will mature over time and taste better with keeping.

This cake can be prepared months ahead of time and kept refrigerated. Thaw before serving.

White Chocolate Fruit Cake

Makes two 23-cm round cakes

Dark rum *240 ml*
Walnuts *150 g*
Macadamia nuts *150 g*
Plain (all-purpose) flour *200 g*
Baking powder *1 tsp*
Bicarbonate of soda *½ tsp*
Ground almonds *100 g*
Unsalted butter *180 g, softened*
Golden castor sugar *100 g*
Freshly squeezed orange juice *250 ml*
Mixed spice *1 tsp*
Ground cinnamon *1 tsp*
Orange zest *2 tsp*
Honey *4 Tbsp*
White couverture chocolate buttons *300 g*
Eggs *4, large, at room temperature, beaten*

DRIED FRUIT

Dried cranberries *250 g, chopped*
Dried apricots *250 g*
Raisins *250 g*
Pitted prunes *150 g, chopped*

- Soaked dried fruit overnight in rum.
- Preheat oven to 160°C and roast walnuts and macadamia nuts for 10 minutes. Leave to cool completely before grinding coarsely.
- Decrease oven heat to 150°C. Line two 23-cm round cake pans, leaving a 3-cm overhang all around. Grease lined pans. Prepare another 2 larger pans that will accommodate the 23-cm cake pans for baking using the water bath method.
- Sift flour, baking powder and bicarbonate of soda 3 times. Add ground almonds to mix.
- In a heavy-bottomed saucepan over medium heat, combine butter, sugar, soaked dried fruit, orange juice, mixed spice, ground cinnamon, orange zest, honey and white chocolate. Bring to a boil, then let mixture simmer for about 15 minutes. Remove from heat and set aside for 10 minutes.
- Add beaten eggs, flour mixture and ground nuts to butter mixture. Mix thoroughly using a wooden spoon.
- Pour batter into lined 23-cm cake pans, then place into larger pans. Carefully fill larger pans with warm water until water level is halfway up the sides of smaller pan. Bake for 2 hours 30 minutes or until a skewer inserted into the centre of cakes comes out clean. Remove from oven and leave cakes to cool completely in pans placed on a wire rack.
- Remove cakes from pans. Turn cakes over and peel off greaseproof paper. Make holes all over cakes using a skewer. Drizzle with 2 Tbsp rum and repeat every other day. Wrap cakes with clean greaseproof paper, followed by aluminium foil to keep them moist.
- This cake can be kept for months in a cool, dark place or frozen. Drizzle with rum periodically.
- Slice cake thinly when serving as it is very rich.

NOTE: Feel free to make any substitution to the ingredients as you wish. For example, swap the white chocolate with dark chocolate, but keep the quantity as stated in the recipe.

This cake can be covered with melted chocolate, marzipan or fondant icing, if desired.

Add an attractive sheen to the cake by brushing it with a thin layer of apricot jam. To do this, first heat, then strain the apricot jam. Decorate with chocolate-coated raisins or edible sugar bits, if desired.

SUPER SCRUMPTIOUS

BROWNIES

Orange Chocolate Chip Brownies with Chocolate Frosting *124*

Triple Chocolate Brownies *127*

Nutty Banana Brownies *128*

Blackberry and Macadamia Brownies *130*

Classic Black and White Brownies *133*

Dried Fruit Brownies *134*

CHEESE CAKES

Poached Pear Cheesecake *136*

Honey Lemon Cheesecake *139*

Chilled Pandan Avocado Cheesecake *140*

Orange Chocolate Chip Brownies with Chocolate Frosting

Makes one 23-cm square cake

Plain (all-purpose) flour *150 g*

Baking powder *1½ tsp*

Cocoa powder *50 g*

Salt *½ tsp*

Ground almonds *50 g*

Unsalted butter *250 g, softened*

Light brown sugar *220 g*

Eggs *6, medium, at room temperature*

Vanilla extract *1 Tbsp*

Orange *1, grated for zest and squeezed for juice; reserve 1 tsp zest for garnishing*

Chocolate chips *100 g + more for garnishing*

CHOCOLATE FROSTING

Couverture milk chocolate droplets *200 g*

Whipping cream *4 Tbsp*

Orange liqueur (optional) *1 tsp*

- Preheat oven to 160°C. Grease and line a 23-cm square cake pan with greaseproof paper, leaving an overhang on two opposite sides.
- Sift flour, baking powder, cocoa powder and salt together once. Add ground almonds and mix well.
- Using an electric mixer with a paddle attachment, cream butter at medium speed for 1 minute. Add sugar and beat for another minute.
- Add eggs one at a time and beat until incorporated. Add vanilla extract, orange zest and juice and beat for another minute to combine.
- Gradually add flour mixture and continue to beat for another minute at low speed.
- Stir in chocolate chips and mix well.

NOTE: When testing if brownies are done, a skewer inserted into the centre of the cake may not turn out clean as the skewer may have penetrated some melted chocolate chips. The best way to do this test is to clean the skewer and insert it into different parts of the brownie.

- Pour batter into cake pan and bake for 45–50 minutes or until the cake springs back when lightly touched.
- Remove from oven. Leave cake to cool completely in pan placed on a wire rack.
- Remove brownie from the cake pan by gently lifting both sides of the greaseproof paper. Pour chocolate frosting over brownie, top with chocolate chips and a sprinkling of orange zest.
- To make chocolate frosting, place couverture and whipping cream in a heatproof bowl and microwave for 1 minute on High. Take care not to burn the couverture. The couverture should be melting and the cream warm. Remove from microwave oven and stir the mixture to combine. Stir in orange liqueur, if desired.

Triple Chocolate Brownies

Makes one 23-cm square cake

Self-raising flour *90 g*
Baking powder *½ tsp*
Salt *a pinch*
Unsweetened bitter chocolate buttons *200 g*
Unsalted butter *150 g, softened*
Eggs *2, large, at room temperature*
Castor sugar *160 g*
Vanilla extract *1 tsp*
Semi-sweet milk chocolate buttons *100 g*
White chocolate chips *100 g*
Cocoa powder *4 Tbsp, sifted*

- Preheat oven to 180°C. Line and grease a 23-cm square cake pan with greaseproof paper, leaving an overhang on two opposite sides.
- Sift flour, baking powder and salt once.
- Place unsweetened bitter chocolate buttons and butter in a double boiler or a bowl set over simmering water and stir over medium heat until melted. Set aside.
- Using an electric mixer with a paddle attachment, beat eggs and sugar at medium-high speed for about 3 minutes until incorporated. Drizzle in melted chocolate and butter mixture and vanilla extract.
- Add flour mixture to combine. Finally, add milk chocolate buttons and white chocolate chips.
- Pour batter into prepared cake pan and bake for about 30 minutes or until cake is just set. The centre may still be a little wobbly.
- Remove from oven and leave to cool completely in pan placed on a wire rack. Takes about 1 hour.
- Remove brownie from cake pan by gently lifting both sides of greaseproof paper. Dust brownie with cocoa powder, slice and serve.

NOTE: This brownie has a crisp top and soft centre.

Brownies can be kept in airtight containers in the refrigerator for up to a month. Heat in the microwave oven for 30 seconds to 1 minute before serving.

Nutty Banana Brownies

Makes one 23-cm square cake

Self-raising flour 100 g
Baking powder 1 tsp
Cocoa powder 100 g
Salt ½ tsp
Unsalted butter 150 g
Light brown sugar 150 g
Fresh milk 70 ml
Eggs 3, medium, at room temperature
Ripe bananas 5, medium; 3 peeled and mashed; 2 peeled, sliced and coated with 2 Tbsp flour
Vanilla extract 1 tsp
Rose water 1 tsp
Almond nibs 150 g
Icing sugar or snow powder as needed

- Preheat oven to 180°C. Line a 23-cm square cake pan with aluminium foil, leaving an overhang on two opposite sides. Make sure to push the aluminium foil right down to the corners of the cake pan, so the shape of the brownie will not be affected. Butter the foil lightly and line the cake pan again with greaseproof paper.
- Sift flour, baking powder, cocoa powder and salt together once.
- Using a heavy-bottomed saucepan over medium heat, stir butter, sugar and milk until melted and smooth. Remove from heat.
- Stir in eggs, mashed bananas, vanilla extract and rose water and mix well.

NOTE: For a richer flavour, replace the light brown sugar with light muscovado sugar.

This brownie can be wrapped in aluminium foil and stored in the refrigerator for up to a week. Heat in the microwave oven for 30 seconds to 1 minute before serving.

- Add sifted flour mixture to combine.
- Fold in flour-coated bananas and almond nibs.
- Pour batter into cake pan and bake for about 30 minutes or until brownie is firm to the touch.
- Remove from oven. Leave brownie to cool completely in pan placed on a wire rack.
- Remove brownie from the cake pan by gently lifting both sides of aluminium foil. Wrap the brownie with aluminium foil and refrigerate for a few hours until firm.
- Before serving, sprinkle with icing sugar or snow powder.

Blackberry and Macadamia Brownies

Makes one 23-cm square cake

Plain (all-purpose) flour *180 g*
Baking powder *1 tsp*
Cocoa powder *50 g*
Salt *½ tsp*
Unsalted butter *250 g, softened*
Light brown sugar *200 g*
Rose water *1½ tsp*
Eggs *4, medium, at room temperature*
Macadamia nuts *100 g, roasted and coarsely chopped*
Fresh blackberries *300 g, washed and drained*

TOPPING

Dark chocolate *150 g, chopped*
Unsalted butter *50 g*
Vanilla extract *1 tsp*
Whole macadamia nuts *as desired*
Fresh blackberries *as desired*

- Preheat oven to 180°C. Line a 23-cm square cake pan with aluminium foil, leaving an overhang on two opposite sides. Make sure to push the aluminium foil right down to the corners of the cake pan, so the shape of the brownie will not be affected. Butter the foil lightly and line the cake pan again with greaseproof paper.
- Sift flour, baking powder, cocoa powder and salt together once.
- Using an electric mixer with a paddle attachment, cream butter, sugar and rose water at medium speed for 1 minute. Add eggs one at a time and beat until incorporated. Add flour mixture and beat for about 1 minute.
- Remove mixing bowl from mixer. Using a wooden spoon, stir in nuts and blackberries. Mix until smooth.
- Pour batter into prepared cake pan and smoothen the surface slightly using the back of a metal spoon dipped first in water.

NOTE: Should the centre of the brownie sink after baking, press the sides down gently while the cake is still warm to level the brownie.

- Place cake pan on the centre rack of the oven and bake for 35–40 minutes or until cake is set. Brownie will be slightly fudgy in the centre.
- Remove from oven and leave brownie to cool in pan placed on a wire rack. Takes about 1 hour.
- Once cool, remove brownie from cake pan by gently lifting both sides of aluminium foil. Wrap brownie in aluminium foil and refrigerate for a few hours until firm.
- Prepare topping. Using a double boiler or a bowl set over simmering water, stir dark chocolate, butter and vanilla extract over medium heat until chocolate and butter are melted and smooth. Leave to cool slightly and spread over brownie. Decorate with macadamia nuts and blackberries before cutting to serve.

Classic Black and White Brownies

Makes one 23-cm square cake

CLASSIC BLACK
Plain (all-purpose) flour *120 g*
Double-action baking powder *1 tsp*
Salt *½ tsp*
Unsalted butter *150 g, softened*
Unsweetened bitter chocolate buttons *125 g*
Light muscovado sugar *200 g*
Vanilla extract *1 tsp*
Eggs *2, large, at room temperature*

CLASSIC WHITE
Cream cheese *265 g, softened*
Castor sugar *90 g*
Lemon zest *1½ Tbsp*
Freshly squeezed lemon juice *3 Tbsp*
Vanilla extract *2 tsp*
Fresh milk *3 Tbsp*
Cornflour *2 tsp*
Egg *1, large, at room temperature*
Egg yolk *1, large, at room temperature*
Light sour cream *50 ml*

CREAM CHEESE FROSTING
Cream cheese *250 g, softened*
Unsalted butter *125 g, softened*
Icing sugar *100 g*
Vanilla extract *1 tsp*

- Preheat oven to 170°C. Line a 23-cm square cake pan with aluminium foil, leaving an overhang on two opposite sides. Make sure to push the aluminium foil right down to the corners of the cake pan, so the shape of the brownie will not be affected. Butter the foil lightly and line the cake pan again with greaseproof paper.

- Prepare classic black layer. Sift flour, baking powder and salt together once. Using a double boiler over low heat, stir butter and chocolate buttons together until melted and smooth. Takes 3–5 minutes. Remove from heat, then stir in sugar and vanilla extract using a wooden spoon. Add eggs one at a time until incorporated. Sift in flour mixture and mix until batter is smooth and glossy. Set aside.

- Prepare classic white layer. Using an electric mixer with a paddle attachment, beat cream cheese and sugar until creamy. Takes about 4 minutes. Beat in lemon zest, lemon juice and vanilla extract for 1 minute. Add milk and cornflour and beat until blended. Add egg, then egg yolk, and beat until incorporated. Finally add sour cream and beat until mixed. Set aside.

NOTE: When using chocolate in baking, always use the best quality you can find as it will affect the taste of the final product.

Give this brownie an extra punch by adding 1 Tbsp rum to the classic black layer. Add it to the batter together with the vanilla extract.

- Pour classic black batter into prepared cake pan. Smoothen the surface slightly with the back of a metal spoon dipped first in water. Pour classic white batter over.

- Place cake pan on the lower rack of the oven and bake for about 55 minutes. Reduce temperature to 130°C and bake for another 15–20 minutes or until cake is risen around the edges and centre is almost set.

- Remove from oven. Leave brownie to cool in pan placed on a wire rack. Takes about 1 hour.

- Once cool, remove brownie from the cake pan by gently lifting both sides of aluminium foil. Wrap brownie in aluminium foil and refrigerate overnight.

- Prepare cream cheese frosting. Beat cream cheese until softened. Add unsalted butter and beat until incorporated. Add icing sugar and beat until light. Add vanilla extract and beat well.

- Cover brownie with cream cheese frosting and dust lightly with cocoa powder, if desired.

Dried Fruit Brownies

Makes one 23-cm square cake

Plain (all-purpose) flour *120 g*

Baking powder *1 tsp*

Salt *½ tsp*

Freshly squeezed orange juice *4 Tbsp*

Unsweetened chocolate *120 g, melted*

Unsalted butter *160 g, softened*

Golden castor sugar *150 g*

Eggs *2, large, at room temperature*

Vanilla extract *1 tsp*

Rose water *1 tsp*

Ground cinnamon *½ tsp*

DRIED FRUIT

Dried mangoes *100 g, diced*

Dried apricots *100 g, diced*

Golden raisins *60 g, diced*

Pitted prunes *60 g, diced*

Dried figs *30 g, diced*

Dried cranberries *30 g, diced*

CHOCOLATE GLAZE

Bittersweet chocolate *200 g, chopped*

Unsalted butter *160 g*

Corn syrup *1 Tbsp*

- Preheat oven to 180°C. Line a 23-cm square cake pan with aluminium foil, leaving an overhang on two opposite sides. Make sure to push the aluminium foil right down to the corners of the cake pan, so the shape of the brownie will not be affected. Butter the foil lightly and line the cake pan again with greaseproof paper.
- Sift flour, baking powder and salt together once.
- Soak dried fruit in freshly squeezed orange juice.
- Place unsweetened chocolate in a microwave-safe bowl and heat in the microwave oven for 30 seconds on High. Remove and stir chocolate, then return to microwave oven and heat for another 30 seconds until completely melted. Set aside.
- Using an electric mixer with a paddle attachment, beat butter and sugar for 3 minutes.
- Add eggs one at a time and beat for 20 seconds after each addition.
- Add vanilla extract, rose water and ground cinnamon and beat to mix.
- Add melted chocolate and mix well.
- Pour in all the flour mixture at once and beat for 1 minute.
- Add soaked dried fruit and mix thoroughly.
- Pour batter into prepared cake pan and smoothen the surface slightly with the back of a metal spoon dipped first in water.
- Place cake pan on the centre rack of the oven and bake for about 50 minutes or until cake is set.
- Remove from oven. Leave brownie to cool in pan placed on a wire rack. Takes about 1 hour.
- Once cool, remove brownie from the cake pan by gently lifting both sides of aluminium foil.
- Cream brownie with chocolate glaze, then sprinkle some dried mixed fruit over the top. Wrap with aluminium foil and refrigerate overnight.
- To prepare chocolate glaze, place bittersweet chocolate, butter and corn syrup in a double boiler over low heat or in a bowl set over simmering water. Stir until chocolate is melted. Do not over heat. Remove glaze from heat and stir again until smooth. Cool glaze before using.

NOTE: This brownie can be wrapped in aluminium foil and stored in the refrigerator for up to a week. Heat in the microwave oven for 30 seconds to 1 minute before serving.

If preferred, omit the chocolate glaze, dust brownie with icing sugar and decorate with fruit of choice before serving.

Poached Pear Cheesecake

Makes one 23-cm square cheesecake

BASE
Digestive biscuits *200 g, crushed*
Unsalted butter *100 g, melted*

FILLING
Cream cheese *550 g, softened*
Golden castor sugar *130 g*
Cornflour *2 Tbsp*
Vanilla extract *3 tsp*
Freshly squeezed lemon juice *1 tsp*
Lemon zest *1 tsp*
Eggs *2, medium, at room temperature*
Egg yolk *1, medium, at room temperature*
Light sour cream *4 Tbsp*
Whipping cream *4 Tbsp*
Pears *3, peeled and cored*

POACHED PEARS
Water *750 ml*
Castor sugar *280 g*
Freshly squeezed orange juice *250 ml*
Pears *4, peeled, cored and quartered*
Cinnamon stick *1*
Whole cloves *2*
Black peppercorns *a few*
Lemon *1, halved*
Vanilla bean *1, split lengthwise*
Star anise *2*
Ginger *10 slices*
Lemon *1, grated for zest*
Honey *2 Tbsp*
Raisins or dried cranberries (optional) *120 g*

- Grease a 23-cm square springform pan. Wrap the outside of pan with 2 layers of aluminium foil, covering the bottom and sides of pan.
- Place crushed digestive biscuits and melted butter into a mixing bowl and mix well. Press mixture into the base of prepared springform pan and refrigerate for about 2 hours.
- Prepare poached pears. In a large saucepan over medium heat, boil water and sugar until sugar dissolves. Add rest of ingredients, except raisins or cranberries. Reduce heat to low and cover saucepan, leaving a small gap. Simmer for about 25 minutes until pear is tender and cooked. Remove from heat and let pear cool in liquid. While liquid is still warm, add raisins or cranberries, if desired. Set aside. Drain pears and raisins or cranberries well before using.
- Preheat oven to 160°C.
- Prepare filling. Using an electric mixer with a paddle attachment, beat cream cheese at medium speed for about 4 minutes until soft. Add sugar and beat for another 3 minutes. Add cornflour, vanilla extract, lemon juice and zest and beat until incorporated.

NOTE: When poaching the pears, add a touch of festivity by substituting the water and orange juice with 500 ml water and 500 ml white wine (sweet or dry) or sparkling cider, or 750 ml red wine and 250 ml water.

- Add eggs and egg yolk one at a time and beat for 30 seconds after each addition. Stop and scrape down the sides of the bowl. Beat in sour cream and whipping cream to mix. Do not overbeat.
- Gently pour half the batter into springform pan, arrange poached pears, together with raisins or cranberries, in a row over batter, then top with remaining batter.
- Place springform pan into a larger shallow pan and fill shallow pan with boiling water until three-quarters up the sides of springform pan. Bake for about 1 hour 15 minutes or until top of cake is slightly golden. Turn off oven and leave cake to sit in warm oven for 2 hours with oven door slightly ajar.
- Remove cake from water bath. Peel off foil. Leave cake in springform pan and cover with plastic wrap. Refrigerate overnight.
- To unmould cake, run a sharp knife around the sides of pan. Release catch on side of pan, then lift cake out of the ring. Insert a metal palette knife under the base of cake and move in a slow circular motion. Lift cake from base of pan onto a serving plate.
- Slice cake using a warm serrated knife. Wipe knife clean, then repeat to heat knife before cutting the next piece.

Honey Lemon Cheesecake

Makes one 23-cm round cheesecake

DIGESTIVE BISCUIT BASE
Digestive biscuits *200 g, crushed*
Unsalted butter *100 g, melted*

FILLING
Cream cheese *650 g, softened*
Castor sugar *80 g*
Honey *80 ml*
Cornflour *4 Tbsp*
Lemons *2, finely grated for zest, then squeezed for 4 tsp juice*
Vanilla extract *4 tsp*
Eggs *3, medium, at room temperature*
Light sour cream *160 ml*
Whipping cream *70 ml*

TOPPING
Honey *as needed*
Lemon slices or roasted nuts of choice *as needed*

- Preheat oven to 160°C. Grease a 23-cm round springform pan. Wrap the outside of pan with aluminium foil, covering the bottom and sides of pan.
- Place crushed digestive biscuits and melted butter into a mixing bowl and mix well. Press mixture into the base of prepared springform pan and chill for 3 hours.
- Using an electric mixer with a paddle attachment, beat cream cheese, sugar and honey at medium speed for about 5 minutes until light. Scrape down the sides of bowl. Blend in cornflour and lemon zest to combine. Add vanilla extract and lemon juice. Reduce speed to low, add eggs one at a time and beat for 30 seconds after each addition. Finally add sour cream and whipping cream and beat to incorporate.

NOTE: Should there be excess batter, pour it into small aluminium cups and place in the oven to bake together with the large cake.

- Spoon filling into springform pan. Place springform pan into a larger shallow pan and fill shallow pan with boiling water until three-quarters up the sides of springform pan. Bake for 1 hour 20 minutes or until top of cake is golden. Turn off oven and leave cake to sit in warm oven for 2 hours with oven door slightly ajar.
- Remove cake from water bath. Peel off foil. Leave cake in springform pan and cover with plastic wrap. Refrigerate overnight.
- To serve, let cake stand at room temperature for 20 minutes. To unmould cake, run a sharp knife around the sides of pan. Release catch on side of pan, then lift cake out of the ring. Insert a metal palette knife under the base of cake and move in a slow circular motion. Lift cake from base of pan onto a serving plate.
- Drizzle top of cake with honey and decorate with lemon slices or nuts, if desired.

Chilled Pandan Avocado Cheesecake

Makes two 23-cm round cheesecakes

PANDAN CAKE BASE

Self-raising flour *200 g*
Unsalted butter *230 g*
Golden castor sugar *230 g*
Eggs *5, large, at room temperature*
Vanilla extract *1 tsp*
Freshly squeezed orange juice *1 Tbsp*
Fresh milk *1 Tbsp*
Coconut milk *2 Tbsp*
Pandan paste *2 tsp*

FILLING

Ripe avocados *2, peeled and stone removed*
Fresh milk *1 Tbsp*
Cream cheese *350 g*
Castor sugar *70 g*
Freshly squeezed orange juice *2 Tbsp + 150 ml*
Gelatine powder *6 tsp*
Whipping cream *250 ml*

- Preheat oven to 180°C. Grease and line a 23-cm round cake pan.
- Sift flour 3 times. Set aside.
- Using an electric mixer with a paddle attachment, beat butter for 1 minute. Add sugar, then cream for about 12 minutes until pale and creamy. Add eggs one at a time and beat to incorporate after each addition. Add vanilla extract, orange juice, milk, coconut milk and pandan paste and mix well. Fold flour in by the spoonful until smooth.
- Spoon batter into cake pan and bake for 45 minutes or until a skewer inserted into centre of cake comes out clean. Leave cake in pan for 5 minutes before removing to cool completely on a wire rack. When cake is cool, cut horizontally in half and trim to fit into base of 2 springform pans. Set aside.
- Prepare filling. Place avocado and milk in a blender and blend into a smooth paste. Measure out 180 g avocado paste.
- Using an electric mixer with a paddle attachment, beat cream cheese and sugar at medium-high speed for about 6 minutes until light and creamy. Add 2 Tbsp orange juice and beat for 30 seconds.

- Sprinkle gelatine over 150 ml orange juice placed in a double boiler or bowl set over simmering water and heat for about 3 minutes or until gelatine is dissolved.
- Pour gelatine mixture into cream cheese mixture and continue to beat at low speed for 3 minutes. Add 180 g avocado paste and beat to mix well. Set aside.
- Meanwhile, in a clean mixing bowl with a whisk attachment, whisk whipping cream for about 3 minutes until soft peaks form.
- Add avocado mixture into whipped cream and mix well. The mixture will reduce in volume. Pour mixture evenly in the 2 prepared springform pans. Smoothen surface and chill cakes overnight.
- To unmould cakes, run a sharp knife around the side of each pan. Release catch on side of each pan, then lift cake out of ring. Insert a metal palette knife under the base of cake and move in a slow circular motion. Lift cake from base of pan onto a serving plate.
- Decorate cakes with whipped cream and slices of avocado, if desired. Refrigerate to chill before serving.

NOTE: Chilled cheesecakes are best eaten a day old. Do not keep for more than 2 days.

As a variation to this recipe, replace the cake base with a digestive biscuit base (page 139).

WEIGHTS AND MEASURES

Quantities for this book are given in Metric and American (spoon and cup) measures. Standard spoon and cup measurements used are: 1 teaspoon = 5 ml, 1 tablespoon = 15 ml, 1 cup = 250 ml. All measures are level unless otherwise stated.

LIQUID & VOLUME MEASURES

Metric	Imperial	American
5 ml	1/6 fl oz	1 teaspoon
10 ml	1/3 fl oz	1 dessertspoon
15 ml	1/2 fl oz	1 tablespoon
60 ml	2 fl oz	1/4 cup (4 tablespoons)
85 ml	2 1/2 fl oz	1/3 cup
90 ml	3 fl oz	3/8 cup (6 tablespoons)
125 ml	4 fl oz	1/2 cup
180 ml	6 fl oz	3/4 cup
250 ml	8 fl oz	1 cup
300 ml	10 fl oz (1/2 pint)	1 1/4 cups
375 ml	12 fl oz	1 1/2 cups
435 ml	14 fl oz	1 3/4 cups
500 ml	16 fl oz	2 cups
625 ml	20 fl oz (1 pint)	2 1/2 cups
750 ml	24 fl oz	3 cups
1 litre	32 fl oz	4 cups
1.25 litres	40 fl oz (2 pints)	5 cups
1.5 litres	48 fl oz	6 cups
2.5 litres	80 fl oz (4 pints)	10 cups

DRY MEASURES

Metric	Imperial
30 grams	1 ounce
45 grams	1 1/2 ounces
55 grams	2 ounces
70 grams	2 1/2 ounces
85 grams	3 ounces
100 grams	3 1/2 ounces
110 grams	4 ounces
125 grams	4 1/2 ounces
140 grams	5 ounces
280 grams	10 ounces
450 grams	16 ounces, 1 pound
500 grams	1 pound, 1 1/2 ounces
700 grams	1 1/2 pounds
800 grams	1 3/4 pounds
1 kilogram	2 pounds, 3 ounces
1.5 kilograms	3 pounds, 4 1/2 ounces
2 kilograms	4 pounds, 6 ounces

OVEN TEMPERATURE

	°C	°F	Gas Regulo
Very slow	120	250	1
Slow	150	300	2
Moderately slow	160	325	3
Moderate	180	350	4
Moderately hot	190/200	370/400	5/6
Hot	210/220	410/440	6/7
Very hot	230	450	8
Super hot	250/290	475/550	9/10

LENGTH

Metric	Imperial
0.5 cm	1/4 inch
1 cm	1/2 inch
1.5 cm	3/4 inch
2.5 cm	1 inch

The publisher wishes to thank Kirby Kwek, owner of Stew-arts, for the use of his warehouse premises for the photography session; and Sanae Inada Wallwork, Lee Mei Lin and Violet Phoon for the loan of the tableware used in this book.

Editor: Lydia Leong
Designer: Lynn Chin

All photography by Joshua Tan, Elements By The Box;
except author's photo by Ng Chai Soong

First published 2011
This new edition 2019
Published by Marshall Cavendish Cuisine
An imprint of Marshall Cavendish International

Copyright © 2011 Marshall Cavendish International (Asia) Private Limited

All rights reserved

No part of this publication may be reproduced, stored in a retrieval system or transmitted, in any form or by any means, electronic, mechanical, photocopying, recording or otherwise, without the prior permission of the copyright owner. Requests for permission should be addressed to the Publisher, Marshall Cavendish International (Asia) Private Limited, 1 New Industrial Road, Singapore 536196. Tel: (65) 6213 9300
E-mail: genref@sg.marshallcavendish.com Website: www.marshallcavendish.com/genref

Limits of Liability/Disclaimer of Warranty: The Author and Publisher of this book have used their best efforts in preparing this book. The parties make no representation or warranties with respect to the contents of this book and are not responsible for the outcome of any recipe in this book. While the parties have reviewed each recipe carefully, the reader may not always achieve the results desired due to variations in ingredients, cooking temperatures and individual cooking abilities. The parties shall in no event be liable for any loss of profit or any other commercial damage, including but not limited to special, incidental, consequential, or other damages.

Other Marshall Cavendish Offices:
Marshall Cavendish Corporation, 99 White Plains Road, Tarrytown NY 10591-9001, USA • Marshall Cavendish International (Thailand) Co Ltd, 253 Asoke, 12th Flr, Sukhumvit 21 Road, Klongtoey Nua, Wattana, Bangkok 10110, Thailand • Marshall Cavendish (Malaysia) Sdn Bhd, Times Subang, Lot 46, Subang Hi-Tech Industrial Park, Batu Tiga, 40000 Shah Alam, Selangor Darul Ehsan, Malaysia.

Marshall Cavendish is a registered trademark of Times Publishing Limited

National Library Board, Singapore Cataloguing-in-Publication Data

Name: Teoh, Allan Albert.
Title: AllanBakes really good cakes : with tips and tricks for successful baking / Allan Albert Teoh.
Description: Singapore : Marshall Cavendish Cuisine, 2019.
Identifier(s): OCN 1110686493 | ISBN 978-981-48-6828-0 (paperback)
Subject(s): LCSH: Cake.
Classification: DDC 641.8653--dc23

Printed in Singapore